# LEADERSHIP,
# ASSHOLES,
# BLOCKCHAIN
and
# YOU

# LEADERSHIP, ASSHOLES, BLOCKCHAIN

and

# YOU

Jan Nyholm

Cover design and interior formatting by Andy Meaden / meadencreative.com

This book is written to my daughter Venezia for her 18th birthday; an amazing young woman who, along with other young people, will hopefully be inspired to shape the world in a better way than my generation has done.

# CONTENTS

# PREFACE

It was not my initial intention to write a book. On a trip to Bhutan in October 2017 I met Avi, a consultant. We ended up having many great conversations in which we exchanged our stories from business life. At some point Avi looked at me and said 'Jan, you need to write your stories down and publish a book'. I had no ambition to write a book, but after contemplating it for five months, I felt inspired to write my stories down – for my daughter. I wanted her to gain an understanding of business life, for better or worse. I wanted her to understand what had given me passion and why I had chosen to do what I did. I wanted her to see what kind of people inspired me in my work and what kind of people I wish I had not come across. I wanted to openly share my successes and failures, in the hope that she could learn something from them. And most importantly, I wanted to inspire her to be true to herself and follow her passion.

After finishing writing my stories, I felt good. It had helped me reflect on many things and strengthened my beliefs in what is right and wrong. I shared my writing with a few friends who kindly encouraged me to make a book out of it. OK, I thought, but who wants to read about my experiences? Realizing that I had clearly pointed out who, for me, were great leaders, as well as managers behaving like assholes, I decided to write a second part on great leadership, with the hope of inspiring people to think like great leaders... rather than being assholes. After finishing that part, I realized there are so many books on leadership and mine would contribute nothing if I did not write about what great leaders must do, what challenges the world faces that need to be solved by great leaders. So, I set out to write the third part of the book about the challenges the world faces, with a focus on what I truly believe is our biggest challenge: income and wealth inequality. This allowed me to incorporate my current passion for new technologies, especially Blockchain, as they stand to change the world in unimaginable ways – for better and worse. It further allowed me to analyze issues I feel strongly about such as education in a tech-driven world, what companies are for, and wealth distribution policies. Through the work, I found we have solutions at hand but simply ignore them. I was about to end the book after calling out world leaders to stand up and do the right things to solve the world's most pressing problems.

But then I read a newspaper article, referred to in the book, that made me lose my belief that world leaders will stand up and solve these problems. That lead me to look at myself, or rather all of us. It is us who are required to stand up to ensure solutions to the world's most pressing problems are found – we cannot simply wait for someone else to do it. So, I set out to write the fourth part of the book, which allowed me to bring to light how we are often our own worst enemy and how we as humans live our lives way below our potential. As I have met many great conscious people the last few years who have inspired me, I enthusiastically decided to write about human mankind, how we think, or don't, and why we are facing severe problems to begin with. It allowed me to energize myself and start believing that it is in our hands to make the world a better place and that it is doable. It allowed me to try to inspire YOU, the reader, to stand up and be part of that change.

You might like the book, you might agree or disagree with my view points, but I sincerely hope the book will change something in you, maybe inspiring you to be the best you can be, think like a leader, and live a successful life, while changing the world.

It should be noted that based on legal advice, I have been overly careful in calling assholes, well, assholes, stating names, and sharing shocking stories. But despite this toning down, I hope I have still been able to make my point.

## P.S. Covid-19

Just as I have finished writing this book and am preparing to publish it, the coronavirus has broken out and been labelled a pandemic. My reaction was to write some more, reflecting on this major human social experiment, but soon decided not to. I think the coronavirus proves many of the points I am trying to make in this book. Firstly, we see how technology and digitalization is making a huge leap forward and plays an important and positive part in solving problems created by the virus. Secondly, we clearly see how some people behave like assholes and run out and buy everything they can, filling up their house, and only thinking about themselves. We see other people that put their lives at risk every day to help those who most need it. We see leaders that politicize the virus for their own re-election benefit and we see leaders that truly stand up, people we had never heard about, and make the talks that the elected leaders fail to do. We see some business leaders that change their firm's production to help fight the virus and other business assholes that try to make huge profits out of the virus. Yes, in the time of crisis, people show their true colors.

I am optimistic that with the virus, we will not go back to how everything used to be. I am optimistic people will start to reflect more on what matters in life and what does not. People will see that we are all dependent on each other, that there is no solution in being selfish. People seem to fear death the most, although it goes hand-in-hand with life and the only thing that is certain in life is death. The coronavirus stokes up this fear of death and makes people either reflective or irrational. Either way, it does put into perspective how we live and maybe how we could or should live. This is a moment for reflection, a chance to question the destructive force of human mankind and a time to start discussing a better way forward for the world and for each of us. We will beat the virus with technology and science, but to avoid other crises, we need to beat the unconscious way of human mankind. It will now be clear to most that the most important thing we have in life is our relationships with other humans and that only together can we all live up to our full potential. The coronavirus is a bad thing with sad consequences, but it might be the change agent we needed. Many times in history humans have had to face a big destructive disruption to be able to take the world to a higher and better standard afterwards. Nothing is so bad that it is not good for something. That might be true for the coronavirus, assuming we all use it as a push to step up. We have all the negative effects of the virus; now let's all ensure we also get substantial positive effects. I will be delighted if, by reading this book, anyone gets inspired to help ensure that happens. So rather than re-writing and adjusting the book, I believe the coronavirus, for better or worse, simply emphasizes most of my key messages.

PREFACE

PREFACE

# PART I

## LEADERS, MANAGERS, AND ASSHOLES

# 1.
# WHAT THEY DON'T TEACH YOU IN BUSINESS SCHOOL

I never doubted I wanted to be in business. Why? No idea, but I did not overly reflect on other options, didn't take career advice from anyone, or subject myself to career assessments in the hopes of discovering what I would be most suited to. I just knew. Perhaps unimpressively, I became one of those who simply followed in the footsteps of their father and, in my case, both of my grandfathers.

Growing up in Denmark, I wanted to attend the Copenhagen Business School. I decided on this in my first year of high-school. Never mind that I had spent the first 10 years of school worrying about one major issue: Were my grades good enough to move up to the next class or would I have to re-do the year? I somehow managed to scrape through by the skin of my teeth – presumably because my teachers didn't want to get me for another year. When the time came to enter Danish high-school after 10th grade, all my teachers agreed: I was simply not qualified. It finally occurred to me that, maybe, I would not be a business man. Perhaps I'd end up being a bus driver. There's nothing wrong with being a bus driver, but it was not what I wanted. *I wanted to drive business, not drive buses.* Luckily, my Dad took charge and threw me in his car one evening. We visited some of my teachers who reluctantly signed a pre-drafted letter stating something similar to 'There might be a theoretical chance Jan could make it, should he be given the chance'. The letters were sent to a family friend who ran a very strict boarding school and, before I knew it, I had started my first year in high-school. As I was already way behind, I had to study relatively hard to catch up. It was here that I saw progress: when I actually studied, I was capable of strong grades like anybody else. Three years later, I graduated in the top 10% of my class so gaining acceptance to business school was a piece of cake. I was confident and armed with youthful vigor, ready to take on the world.

As was typical of business schools, I learnt statistics, economics, accounting, and finance – tools that obviously make sense. In addition, they also try to teach you strategy, marketing, organizational behavior etc., all of which are theories and almost useless in a real-world setting. The good news? I was excellent with numbers and had learned to 'bullshit' my way through those impractical theory classes. Armed with those two skills, I graduated with relatively little effort in the top 10% of my class and could now set my sights on an MBA at an Ivy League school.

The bullshitting? That particular tool was developed during my year of military service – the year between high-school and business school. Let it be known that bullshitting is a resourceful tool that prevents one being stuck with the worst tasks or, alternatively, risk getting recruited for another year as Captain. Unless you wanted to spend an extra year in the military, which I did not, there was much incentive to bullshit your way around everything, so you learn.

\*\*\*

It was the last day of exams at the Copenhagen Business School, I sat with a one-way ticket to New York and contemplated the future. Copenhagen, I felt, in all my arrogance, was simply too small and boring for me. Having lined up a job in New York at one of the largest

Japanese electronics firms, I was all set for the next two years.

My first job was as a sales coordinator. Here, I worked under the head of sales, helping with the planning and administration of sales as well as coordinating the national sales force. Looking back, anyone interested in business should pay dues with a few years in sales. Why? Sales ensures a steady flow of profit into the company and, to put it bluntly, it pays for everything else. To this day, I am amazed at those who look down on this vital function. I've found it's mostly people with fancy titles on their business card, doing some job or other they feel is important. In reality, the sales folk enable these chaps to do whatever they do.

Sales is one of those departments with immediate impact. If they sell too cheaply, margins and profit decrease and some of the fancy people might have to be fired. If Sales sell too few units, revenue and profitability decrease and, again, some of the fancy people have to be fired. I saw first-hand how tough sales can be. But, provided you have the right attitude, it's also pretty fun and fast paced. Sales people tend to have wonderful characters and great stories. We need sales people and they need our support and respect. Remember: sales *is* business, it pays for everything else.

This book is not about sales, but I would be doing a disservice to Ed Mahon if I did not share (at least) one of the experiences at my first job in New York.

In the late 70s, Ed was the number one typewriter salesman at IBM with a sales territory covering half the Empire State building. Ed was an amazing, fun, wonderful nut case. Just as I started my job, the company launched the first electronic typewriter with a 1 K memory (yes, one line of text!). Ed was my coach, teacher and guru. He invited me along to sales calls, demonstrating first-hand the art of selling. One day he took me to a potential buyer at a big firm where Ed started to demonstrate the new electronic typewriter. Shortly into the demonstration, the purchase manager asks if it has a specific feature where one can delete the last typing mistake before it prints. Ed ignored the question and simply continued his demonstration. The purchase manager soon repeated his query, and Ed simply stated he would like to get back to that later. A few minutes later the manager asked again (persistent!) and Ed gave the same answer. At the end of the demonstration, Ed asked the purchase manager what he thought of the typewriter. He said it seems great but again repeated his question. Ed leans back, looks at him and asks if it's really that important? The purchase manager answered yes, quite so. Ed then asked him, given the typewriter has that feature, is that decisive and will he purchase the typewriters? The purchase manger answered yes, and in the next 15 seconds, Ed demonstrates that specific function with ease. We ended up leaving with a massive order. How did he hook the client?

Ed realized the hooking point within minutes, but only used it to close. Brilliant! He explained to me that had he answered immediately, he would not have been sure how to close the potential client, and most likely the purchase manager would have had other questions with the meeting would end up at a stalemate, that is to say 'I'll think about it'. This one meeting saved me reading numerous books on how to close the deal: listen to the prospect. They will literally, and unwittingly, point you in the right direction. There is a reason why we have two ears and only one mouth...

They don't teach this at any business school. Actually, business schools don't cover this topic, despite the fact that a company is nothing without sales.

***

After two years working in the sales department, I was accepted to Columbia Business School, NY to start my MBA. I was on a mission and felt an Ivy League education combined with the city of Manhattan was made for me. I will admit that it was a scary and intimidating experience to be at a prestigious university packed with exceptionally smart, hand-picked people. But as life has always shown, it's not always the smartest nor the most hardworking individual that pulls ahead of the crowd. I've always had a relaxed view of my education and decided that I would never make it to Summa Cum Laude status, more commonly known as the top 1%. No chance, the competition was simply too hard. But, me being me, perhaps if I was smart (not intelligent), I could make it to the Dean's list (top 10% supposedly, or something like that). That would make the best job opportunities somewhat easier to come by. Having heard numerous campus stories about studying 24/7 and still being unable to effectively manage the full workload, I developed a clear strategy. I knew I could only sustain maximum effort for a limited time and chose to do so the first semester. I picked the easiest courses and worked my ass off. I was extremely happy when I made the Dean's list that first semester. I slapped that accolade on my CV and relaxed, with the aim of having fun and enjoying the following semesters. Being somewhat lazy is a privilege because it constantly challenges you on how to cut corners creatively – if you have the smarts to pull it off!

# 2.
# FACTS VERSUS BULLSHIT

I had set out to be an investment banker but after a summer internship, while doing my MBA, I changed my mind. It was the 80s hay day of Wall Street and the movie *Wall Street* had just come out. The movie resolutely pointed out Gordon Gekko's dodgy character but, somehow, in some way, he transcended ordinary 'human' limitations and failings; he became a hero and inspiration, almost like a cult leader for the many con artists lining Wall Street. That basically said it all, for me anyway, and I decided I didn't want to spend my working life with such people.

I decided to go with American Express who was in the process of expanding their business interests in Europe. I found myself working under the CEO for Europe, Middle East and Africa, with exciting projects and killer strategies. One day I was tasked with one of the bigger marketing projects, and I must have impressed someone because shortly after executing that project I was promoted and became the Head of Marketing – an area I had zero clue how to run. Now, American Express is a marketing-driven firm where most of their CEOs climb the ranks through marketing, so I thought, 'why not me?'. Over time, American Express would teach me several important lessons that shaped my business career.

At this time, the Amex card was accepted in less than fifty percent of the places held by its biggest competitor, Visa. However, people paid a yearly fee that was three times higher than Visa. The first lesson I learned was that you don't need the best performing product to win. So, why was Amex successful? It's a customer-focused leadership which understands its customer base and what they're willing to pay for. Any Amex card holder justifies himself paying the high fee due to exceptional service, and yes, Amex provided superior service as it's totally customer centric. On a weekly basis, we heard stories such as employees leaving their relative's wedding to provide customers with replacement cards. Personally, I would have fired the employee for stupidity, but then again, it's not for me to judge how people prioritize their work and private lives. The reality was that customers hardly ever used the excellent services available to them. In the end, it was a status symbol, nothing more, nothing less. Paying your restaurant bill with an Amex card would signal to the waiter, your friends, your date, and everyone else that you were *someone*. Being someone is a never-ending obsession for humans, which Amex exploited to the fullest: First a Green Card, then upgrade to a Gold Card, then a Platinum Card, then a Black Card and so on, always accompanied by higher fees and more exclusivity. Genius!

Look at their historical profitability and you will see a company mastering customer insight (while the core product itself is easily surpassed by the competition). What did I learn from this gem? It's not about the product, stupid! It's about the customer. This is in stark contrast to all the firms who pursue 'the best product' idea.

***

Around the time I became head of marketing, something unusual happened. The CEO of Amex, Aldo, boss to 100,000+ employees, decided that Europe, and Germany in particular, were the most important growth opportunity for Amex outside the US. To exploit that, we were allowed to set our own card fee as well as create our own local TV commercials. Needless to say, up until then, directions were dictated by the HQ – something most American firms still implement to this day.

So here I was, the newly appointed Head of Marketing, with a huge opportunity and challenge landing directly in my lap. I figured the card fee could be decided based on facts. At that time, in Germany alone, we sent out 16 million mailings to households (this was way before the Internet) soliciting the Amex card. This we used to gauge responses to different messages and pricing. We then analyzed the response rate, conversion rate, spending, and default rate and chose the pricing and message that optimized customer profitability. This took around six months, and frankly, it was the easiest part. When it came to the TV commercial however, I was absolutely clueless. I wouldn't have recognized a great commercial if it jumped up and bit my leg so this was a challenge indeed. Ogilvy & Mather were our global advertising agency so I met with them in Germany, putting forth the need for a TV commercial. They seemed intrigued and asked for a briefing. I politely asked what kind of briefing was required and how that related to this. They tried to explain but I failed to provide answers to their basic questions. They were the experts and this is what they did for a living so it shouldn't be too difficult, right? In the end, they reluctantly went ahead without a briefing.

After the fee test and TV commercial were completed, it was time for decisions to be ironed out. Aldo decided that the outcome of these decisions was of the utmost importance, and took the corporate jet to Germany. Since he was going to be present, the CEO of Amex International decided to be there, as well as Tom, the newly appointed Head of Global Marketing.

The CEO of Amex Europe trusted me to do the presentation – there was lot riding on this and I knew it. I walked into the room to present my findings and recommendations, and found myself faced with every important executive from the Amex executive team. I was 30 years old with six months of marketing experience – this should be fun...

I started off my presentation with the different fees we had tested and our conclusions on customer profitability. The data was quite clear, statistically significant, and a decision was made quite quickly. We then moved on to the TV commercial. I refused to present it because I didn't have a clue how to argue for the spot that had been produced. I liked it but that was subjective. Yes, we had conducted focus groups but I failed to see how the results would guarantee we would sell more cards. I asked the advertising agency to present the spot. After viewing the commercial, all hell broke loose. Everybody was kind enough to share their opinion, what they liked and what they didn't. This resulted in a long discussion regarding the actors used in the spot. The Americans argued that they didn't 'look' European. The Europeans argued they did, and the agency insisted they were. I was absolutely flabbergasted. The arguments carried on until Aldo proposed a break. By then, I was relieved as I desperately needed to go to the bathroom.

I find myself standing at the urinal, doing my thing, with Aldo on one side and Tom on the other. As we carried on with our business, Aldo asked Tom what he thought of the TV spot. Tom, as the newly appointed global head of marketing, better have a good answer I thought. To my surprise, Tom simply stated, 'I actually think it's quite good but it could be tightened up a bit.' Over and out. Aldo suggested that Tom share his view when the meeting continued. He did, and with his input, that particular segment of the meeting was concluded.

Later on, I asked the agency what that meant. They said they had no idea. I informed them that we would make a few small changes and send it to New York, stating we had tightened it up. Within three days, the TV spot was approved!

That was a great lesson early on in my career: *If you stick to facts, you can drive executive decisions.* When dealing with soft issues, everybody is entitled to their subjective opinion and you never really know if the decision was right or wrong. I find these are bullshit rules and its typically the most senior executive who gets to decide. I decided the pursuit of facts would be my mantra, and I would need to stay away from soft, wobbly issues like advertising. Looking at the success Amex had, I became fanatical about a certain belief: the key success factor in business is to understand customers better than the competition and use those facts to sell relevant services they are willing to pay a premium for. As this book will illustrate, I have stayed true to these beliefs.

# 3.
# FAILURE – ANOTHER LEARNING CURVE IN THE GAME

Around the same time that I started with Amex in London, my family's company in Denmark ran into severe trouble. I was equipped with an MBA, confident, and passionate about the firm I had grown up with so I decided to spend as much time as possible saving the firm. The company, an office equipment supplier, was founded by my grandfather during the Second World War. The business was well known with many service cars driving around the country, displaying the family name prominently. Eventually, through getting my inheritance upfront and taking out a huge bank loan, I and a successful business man slash family friend bought out my remaining family and set about turning the business around. I spent the next year flying out almost every Friday evening from London to Copenhagen and working through each weekend trying to save that company. Most of the key employees were kind enough to meet me on the weekends to help with the turn-around.

\*\*\*

After a year's hard labor, it seemed we had finally succeeded. Unfortunately, the story doesn't end there. I had overseen one small detail due to my inexperience. My partner, the family friend, had insisted that we use his auditor and his head of finance. Shortly after saving the firm, he invited me to a meeting. As I walked into his office, I could see the Head of Finance and the auditor had been invited too. They presented a report that stated the inventory was worth only half of what was stated on the last accounts and the company was therefore technically undercapitalized. As I had personally gone through the full inventory with the heads of sales, I knew this was incorrect and that I was being played, but I also realized that when the accountant and auditor both state it as a fact there was little I could do. He went on to suggest that each of us could simply put in a substantial amount of capital and the problem would be solved. He, of course, knew I was in no position to do so. As I relayed this, he replied that I should simply give him my shares and he would, in turn, save the company and the employees. If not, the company would fold. I stood up and left the meeting, worried that I had been cornered with no way out. I called a friend from high-school, Morten. Morten was a lawyer who had just joined a large Danish law firm. He told me to stay cool and that any worries or emotions from my side would be unwise. We decided on a strategy – call it a bluff to the max. We scheduled another meeting with my partner and informed him I wouldn't be signing any papers – the idea was to bluff him that we intended on having the firm fold. We pushed the point that I was unwilling to let him win in such an unethical manner. To say he was surprised would be an understatement. He knew I had grown up in the firm and more or less knew every employee there, many of whom had known me since I was a small (cute) child. It was a true family business with under 200 employees. We informed him that we were open to a deal where he could take over the firm, but not one where I lost everything. Eventually, I ended up striking an agreement with the acceptance of the bank, where both I and the firm owed money. I would have to pay *only* part of the loan back, and I estimated it would take me five years.

Here I was, a hot shot with an Ivy League background holding a great job with American Express and having just turned the family firm around, suddenly finding myself broke as a beggar. Residing in London, and having to use a big chunk of your salary every month to pay for your mistake makes you both frustrated and humbled. Since then, I have never borrowed money. I know first-hand what it feels like when others take charge of your financial situation, and it's no picnic. I learned debt is the invention of the devil and, at the same time, realized it was an important experience. Had I succeeded in turning a good profit with the family firm, there's a strong chance I might have become (even more) arrogant and lost a greater amount later on. I gained a world of respect for entrepreneurs who take risks every damn day and keep going after they fail. As I will explain later, when it comes to investing in entrepreneurs, those who have experienced failure usually work ten times harder to succeed. They also tend to be smarter about taking risks than those who succeed or strike it lucky the first time. I learned to be more cautious when partnering up and that money changes people, negatively, in most cases. Again, while I had some experience with dodgy partners, this didn't save me soon enough as will be clear later.

I have relayed this story many a time during job interviews. I have learnt that for great leaders, failure is an acceptable and appreciated learning curve. I have seen many leaders assume only those who do nothing, avoid mistakes. I have also seen managers be fearful of failure. They will avoid hiring people who have failed in the past as the managers could be blamed later should something go wrong. They will do whatever it takes to avoid failing. Leaders are bold and try new things. They push their employees to experiment and they themselves know that only by learning from our mistakes do we improve. I have often interviewed people who claimed they had 20 years of experience, only to learn later they had one and then repeated that for the next 19 years. They didn't push nor try new avenues, and were unwilling to take risks. It is only with risks and failures that we learn and move onto bigger and better things. Great leaders live by that motto: never prevent yourself from taking up an exciting opportunity because you're afraid of failing.

# 4.
# LEADERS VERSUS
# MANAGERS

The European insurance markets were set to deregulate in 1994, which meant these large, inflexible insurance companies were suddenly exposed to some *very* real competition across the borders. This was a threat to the very existence of insurance companies – they were accustomed to regulators dictating pricing for customers, among other things. A German insurance company, Nordstern Colonia, was run by Mr. Kleybolt, a smart CEO in my book. He could see what was coming, and at the same time realized that his large firm was like a tanker – one he couldn't steer left or right within a relatively short period. His solution was to create a new insurance company, TELLIT, set up at arm's length to develop a business model that could compete in a deregulated market. He understood the new company would need to be something alien to the current insurance industry, a full focus on customer centricity. Myself, an Amex colleague and an insurance mathematician, Klaus were offered positions on the management team. Klaus was highly intelligent, with his entire career spanning the insurance industry so he was the most qualified to head the company as CEO. Over the next few years, we developed this insurance company from bare bones up, with a foundation that put the customer in focus. We decided to cut out insurance brokers, as they would be an expensive obstacle between us and the customers. We developed products where the customers only paid for the actual risk they represented, and with that, we could cater to the lower risk segment offering much better prices than our competition. Naturally, our model was highly successful. We managed to merge fact-based customer acquisition activities, with risk management activities, resulting in low cost acquisition of lower risk customers. Take note that this was before the Internet had come around, and it was both a marketers and an actuary's dream.

In addition, we decided to be relatively generous when people made a claim. Most individuals pay their premiums over years and when an accident finally occurs, the insurance industry does anything and everything to avoid paying. We made the choice to trust our customers and treated them with the best possible service, including pay out for claims. This led to great recommendations within their circle of friends, and statistically, their friends were usually on the lower end of the risk spectrum too. We were quite innovative and built an amazing business. Unfortunately, we were acquired by AXA, a French insurance group, and that was the end of it. Anyone who has ever worked for French management will know what I mean...

Looking back, I realized we could have been significantly more successful. As intelligent as Klaus was, in my opinion, he lacked business acumen. Klaus, being an insurance industry expert, was averse to taking risks in any form. He preferred getting solid proof concerning any potential decision making before taking steps to implement the next course of action. I had to continuously explain that if I could prove 'it', I would not be in the position to recommend the course as it would be too late by then. The only way to prove it would be to show a competitor was successful with that given idea and by then it was too late. He was also scared about blowing our budgets. In fact, he was so scared that he would cut the customer acquisition budget at the start of the year. By year's end, we obviously acquired less customers than we should have had but he stood by his decision, emphasizing that we had 'saved costs' up front. Really Klaus?

Some people have a natural inclination for business, some don't. As

I will keep pointing out, this isn't something you learn in school. Either you have an instinct for strategy or not, you're either a marketing genius or not. If you fall in the latter categories (the 'have nots'), hire the best in their respective departments and trust them to do what they do best. Don't hire competent people with specialist skill sets and start second guessing them. Klaus was a manager, not a leader. He wanted to be in on every detail and preferred to make all decisions. As he made all decisions, I requested the highest bonus every year as anything that would have gone wrong, in terms of achieving results, was on his head, and I therefore refused to be punished with a low bonus. As you can probably imagine, these were interesting discussions...

Kleybolt, on the other hand, was the epitome of a real leader. He hired experts and left them to do their jobs. He didn't micro manage nor interfere. He set a clear vision and clear goals. As long as we delivered, he left us alone.

# 5.
# BELIEVE IN WHAT YOU DO, OR QUIT

After the French group AXA took over TELLIT, I accepted an offer from Fidelity Investments to run the European markets. At the time, they were the world's largest asset manager. This was an exciting job with an impressive firm run by the owner, Ned Johnson, and boy was it *run* by him. In short, Ned was a great leader. First off, he always reminded us that we worked with his money – if we spent it, we better make sure it comes back. He illustrated how to handle or, rather, how to avoid spending money on unnecessary things. I estimate that during my time working there in the 90s, he must have been one of the 25 wealthiest people in the US. When he visited Europe, he flew on a normal commercial airline wearing his Nike jacket, Swatch watch and he insisted on staying in a regular hotel room. I found out that my predecessor was fired for booking a suite...

We worked in a very cost-efficient manner, and a big portion of our compensation was in company stocks. My salary was relatively low and when our bonuses arrived, it was in stocks. On top of that, I was offered a loan to purchase more stocks. He wanted us to be fully aligned with the company's visions and goals, and it worked. We became 'wealthy' on paper but had no actual cash for vacation – a very smart move, for Ned anyway. This way, being highly incentivized, we ended up tripling the business in a few years.

Ned had a very inquisitive mind, similar to a five-year-old in a way. When he came to Europe, he always insisted we drive around (in my car no less) to the different countries to save costs. So, there I sat, driving down a German autobahn at 200 km/h with one of America's wealthiest people asking me a billion questions: Where will that truck go? What does it transport? Is the driver German? Why do they build roads there? Why are there...

On, and on, and on. It was a well-known fact if you had a meeting with him that required a decision, it was wise to clear your desk, literally. If not, he would pick up a thing, start to analyze it, most likely take it apart while pondering 'why this?' and 'why that?' I found it fascinating that his mind constantly wanted to learn and as soon as he saw something that didn't work, he wanted to improve it. After a ride in a dirty limousine, he started a limousine service which ended up becoming a global firm. When data transfers became too slow for him, he started COLT, a company responsible for laying down faster fiber optics. Ned was a true entrepreneur, a true leader, and a very down to earth and authentic leader. He also understood the pressures of the job and paid attention to his staff. When things were tough or the markets down, he left us alone as he knew we were having a tough time. He trusted us to do whatever we could to salvage the situation. When things were good with the stock markets up and fast growth in assets under management, he would be all over us to ensure we worked to take advantage of the opportunity. I think most, if not all, managers do the exact opposite. From all the bosses I've worked with and for, Ned is the one I admire the most.

***

It sounds like I was having a fantastic time but not everything was 'hunky dory'. The head of Fidelity International, whom I had to deal with on a weekly basis, was very different. This was the guy, it seemed to me, that went from being pushed around and bullied in the school yard to 'now it's my turn!'. He relished pulling our chains and did everything in his power to put us down. He ensured that there were office politics and shifting favorites, and lived for head games that created an environment managed by fear. The sad truth was that most of my colleagues feared him. Managers who use this tactic to control their departments attract weak people. It is not worth dwelling on the stupidity I witnessed day-in day-out, but it was fascinating that the same firm run by Ned also housed a manager with such opposing management styles. When all was said and done, Fidelity was a roaring success. We were also helped by booming stock markets so the company was flourishing. I enjoyed my job which, among other things, was to get Europeans to invest in stocks – something that was anything but common in the 90s. We pitched our fund manager's skills in picking successful companies, we preached long-term investing, no market timing, cost averaging, and any argument that could be made up for investing in an actively managed fund. I felt good in playing a part that would ensure Europeans had money for their retirement.

In 2000, I decided to leave for two reasons. Firstly, the time had come where I simply could not tolerate working for the head of the international division. What's more, I disrespected my colleagues who swallowed his bullshit year-in year-out. Secondly, I started to lose faith in what we preached. We hired the smartest people from Wharton, Columbia, Harvard, Stanford and trained them as analysts for six years. We then took the best and turned them into fund managers. In the end, half of them beat the index, the other half did not; and it was impossible to predict who would fall into either group. The fund manager who beat the index this year was not guaranteed to beat it next year. *A random walk down Wall Street* a book, published in 1973, describing how you cannot outperform the stock market over time, became very relevant to me. Of all the jobs I've had, I had a passion for what we managed to create. First with Amex getting rid of cash, then TELLIT treating customers with respect, and finally Fidelity helping people secure a better pension. Once I lose passion for my work, I know it is time to move on. With Fidelity, I simply stopped believing that asset managers can consistently outperform the market – our core selling point. I stayed true to myself so I quit.

# 6.
# SPEAK UP

During the year 2000 stock markets were booming and any business which was vaguely associated with the Internet, or added a .com to their company name, became highly valued overnight. I saw how friends became instant millionaires and felt I was missing out. My luck seemed to strike just when I decided I wanted out of Fidelity. I got an offer to run *DLJdirect*, an online stock trading firm. With my newly shattered belief in the capabilities of asset managers, I found it fascinating that the Internet could offer individuals instant information on stocks and markets from the comfort of their own home. With a push of a bottom, you could buy or sell shares. It was the early days of the Internet and it seemed quite revolutionary. I thought, 'I could be part of this' and joined. Business was great and, together with porn, we were the first business models generating profits on the Internet. I could direct my passion into helping individuals understand, research, and trade investments. Competitors put millions into building their brands and I found myself travelling to New York to convince the DLJ board to instead invest millions of dollars in helping our clients to actually become successful. This was important because customer acquisition costs were high so if they completed a few unsuccessful trades only to drop out, we would never make money. By providing deep analysis – thorough data and market information – and investment support, alongside some of the rules that we used in Fidelity for successful investment in funds (long-term, no market timing, etc.), we could turn out smarter investors, improve their performance, and retain them as clients.

I loved the job and was passionate about the concept, but within six months of launching we were sold to Credit Suisse, one of the world's largest banks. I remember calling my wife with news that I would most likely get fired as I was now part of Credit Suisse First Boston, the investment banking arm of Credit Suisse, and it didn't feel like home. I remember sitting in my office, wondering what the hell I should do next. In walks a guy, asking for my name. I stare back and ask him for his. He was Brady Dugan, responsible for Equity and it was clear to me that he would be my boss (he later went on to become the global CEO of the Credit Suisse group). He seemed like a nice guy, and was kind enough to put me on the Executive Management Committee for Europe where I sat and talked numbers in our monthly meetings – numbers that were a fraction of every other department boosting incredible fee income for the bank. I did feel out of place...

***

The market crash occurred in 2001. Internet businesses became worthless and Credit Suisse suffered severe financial losses threatening its very existence. And my job? Well, nobody wanted to trade stocks anymore. I was double exposed as both my job and savings were reliant on the stock markets, and Credit Suisse stock (as a result of the merger I had come to hold quite a bit) fell from CHF 80 to CHF 9. I blamed myself for my blindness, and trust, and I promised myself to never expose both income and assets to the same fate: in this case the stock markets. Since that day, I have barely invested in the stock market.

Credit Suisse had been managed by two former McKinsey partners instead of bankers. Just shortly before D-Day, where the bank would have to take emergency measures, a very experienced banker by the name of 'Ossi', was appointed CEO together with a senior investment banker, John, who became CEO of Credit Suisse

First Boston. Their job was to save the bank, and I couldn't believe my luck when I was asked to join the Executive Board for what became a three-year turn-around.

Having prided myself on being totally customer-centric, I was very excited to join what represented the pedigree of customer focus (for me anyway): private banking. A business where people trust their most valuable possessions: their money (I know it should have been their kids but I have learned that they're often not what rich people value the most). A Swiss bank, servicing the wealthiest and most successful people in the world must, I thought, be managed to the highest degree by exceptional leaders. I could not have been more wrong.

Shortly after joining, Ossi decided a larger re-organization should take place to cut costs. He asked me to consider if the marketing division, currently under the Head of Private Banking, should be transferred to my department. I had estimated that the bank spent over $500 million a year on marketing efforts with no coordinated effort, no clear results, and no measured KPIs. We were in a cost-cutting mode and who better than me, a marketing sceptic, to cut costs.

The CEO of Private Banking (call him Hans) hated the idea. One day, as I was in my office on Paradeplatz, Zurich, where the executive board took up the first floor, there was a knock on my door. A stranger walked in. He stated he was on the Executive Board of Private Banking and was here to make sure that the marketing department would not transfer to me. He added that, while I was new here, he and his colleagues had worked with Ossi for over a decade and if I did not agree to abandon the move of marketing they would ensure my time with the company was short-lived. I have seen a lot of bullshit in my time but this was on another level. I invited him to sit down, asked for his business card while taking out my own, and set them down next to each other on the table. I verified we both worked for Credit Suisse, both had very senior positions, and asked if I could assume the major portion of his compensation was in Credit Suisse stocks (like in my case). He confirmed all the above. I then told him to get the hell out of my office, try knocking again, and start over from a position that would help remove the bank from its current situation. As often happens when people play tough and you call their bluff, he got very nervous and insecure before he headed for the door. I told him to sit down and that we should continue, minus the bullshit. He stayed for two and a half hours, after which time we had agreed it made a lot of sense to merge the division with mine.

This did not go down well with his boss, Hans, who demanded a meeting with me. A few days later, I showed up for the meeting and found Hans had been delayed. By a stroke of luck, his Executive Board was present. This provided a fantastic opportunity for me so I told them we could start without Hans. I was lucky that Hans was delayed for 30 minutes because in that time I convinced the Board that the move would be the right thing.

The door flew open, and there Hans stood: a big cigar in hand and waves of arrogance emanating off him. He started to address me, telling me the transfer is not going to happen and this is the last time he will talk about this. He went into a tirade and rambled away. When he finally wore himself out, still standing in the doorway no less, I turned around to his people, thanked them for the meeting and their agreement, and suggested they brief Hans on the outcome. I don't know the specifics but marketing was folded into my department and I managed to cut spending by 60%, saving the bank much needed cash.

I didn't do this on a fluke. This was based on thorough analysis and measuring everything we could think of in terms of the possible business effect of the marketing spend. When a bank is on its knees and the world knows it, when clients have lost a significant amount, there is no point in advertising that we are a great institution. Instead, we should focus on relationship managers that need our help and support to service and retain their clients. When you let 3,000 employees go, mainly fathers with families, there is no point in sponsoring Formula One at $40 million a year to demonstrate teamwork. When relationship managers entertain their clients, there is no point in wining and dining satisfied clients and their spouses. Instead, work on entertaining the difficult clients who complain about everything (even though it makes for a not-as-fun evening). More often than not, they just like the attention. But who are we kidding, no private banker likes taking on those tasks, right? Think outside the box: instead of your client bringing their spouse to an expensive event, have the client bring his or her best friend. There is a high likelihood that person is a potential client. All this might sound logical and straight forward, but in the cozy world of private banking it was as alien as square watermelons in those days.

Swiss private banking secrecy was misused by Swiss banks to help wealthy people avoid taxes in their home countries, and even in some cases help dictators steal money from their countries... Not very honorable, not very fair, and definitely not good for other countries. But for the Swiss, it was a great business model that built the foundations of the banking industry, all based on secrecy. Banks had no need to justify fees or lack of performance; clients were there to save 40% of their fortune in tax. As such, the fact they paid a 1–3% fee and a yearly return was not guaranteed was less important than saving that massive 40% tax. Bankers became complacent and so did the clients. Banks could invent products with high fees and sell these to their (complacent) clients. When performance was abysmal, the markets were to blame. When performance was great, the private banker was highlighted, applauded, and this was used as a selling tool. The few clients that dared to complain were kindly reminded that their money was not taxed (yet)… It's no secret, Swiss private banking business models were successful due to a mis-use of the Swiss banking secrecy rules, and this attracted certain managers. One of my colleagues on the Executive Board shared, 'Jan, you don't get it. Screw the clients, screw the shareholders, we take it all!' Yes, that's exactly what he said.

This business model was highly profitable and allowed the banking sector to pay substantially higher salaries than other industries. If you were head of HR for one of the largest industrial companies, you might make up to $200,000 at that time. That very same job in a big bank would pay you up to $1,000,000. Why? The more you pay your employees, the more you can pay yourself, and banks had the money to play that game where other industries did not. The argument was that if these high salaries were not paid, managers would leave for the competition. In my opinion, as I felt that many of these people lacked integrity, that would be a good thing. The high salaries attract people who prioritize money. They focus on securing the million-dollar bonus rather than doing what is right, they manage and lookout for their careers and bonuses rather than the bank. Money corrupts the weak and most end up selling their souls. Having been born in the 'socialist' society that is Denmark, where everybody is equal and with a culture driven by strong values and beliefs, I struggled. Don't get me wrong, I enjoyed my ridiculously high bonuses but would have been happy with just a quarter of it. I truly believed we did and were doing the wrong thing. The monthly executive board meeting therefore became a problem for me. In banking we have PEP's which are Political Exposed People. They need to be scrutinized and approved by the executive board, so at every board meeting the Head of Private Banking had to present the new PEP clients for approval. I heard about many backgrounds that didn't seem kosher (e.g. the niece of the president of an emerging market with $700m, which she supposedly made through property development at the age of 27...) so I asked questions. Obviously, this was not making me popular. I might be wrong, but I don't remember a single large PEP that was turned down. Why? They were bonus boosters and when shit hits the fan, as you know from the press, some middle manager becomes the scapegoat, with a possible jail term to boot. It was never the top executives back then, a trend we still see to this day.

My experience became everything I despised and I got tired of fighting. *I lost my passion*. I spoke out, brutally honest at all times and knew I was not popular. My Waterloo was the Formula One sponsorship. Sponsorship and its business impact, like advertising, is hard to measure. But then again, most managers don't care. They take pride in seeing their company on TV and a company sponsorship normally reflects the personal interest of the CEO. They enjoy being involved and going to the events. Who wouldn't? In sponsorship and TV advertising, there is no fact-based decision-making taking place. Instead, basic research is used to justify huge expenses: many people saw it, many people loved it, and more remembered it etc. But here are the real questions: How many new customers did we acquire? What volume in additional sales did we generate? These questions are (un) graciously avoided. I have had endless discussions with brand gurus, agencies, and consultants on this theme so let's break it down. The fact that one million + people see your sponsorship or advertising simply means you spent a lot getting it out there. Awareness is easily bought, customers not so much. The fact that a number of crazy women willingly pay several thousand for a hand bag that cost roughly $50 to produce is due to advertising. You do not pay for the bag but the advertising and the expensive high street brand shops that 'urge' you to desire the bag in the first place. Louis Vuitton are the masters of branding and perhaps the one exception that proved me wrong. They have made a brown bag of plastic one of the most desirable items for women all over the world. However, that does not necessarily translate to businesses like banking where a client makes a more conscious decision.

Ossi's passion was Formula One so Credit Suisse sponsored Formula One. As an anecdote, one of my colleagues later became the CEO of an insurance company. He was a passionate soccer fan, so when he joined, the insurance firm started to sponsor soccer. Ossi not only decided to sponsor the Swiss Formula One team Sauber, but also decided that Credit Suisse should buy a significant number of shares in the team. I was vehemently opposed to this as I did not feel we could justify this to our entrenched staff or our clients. The first feedback to the sponsorship I received entirely free. Letters poured in from clients stating they did not want to remain clients at a bank so intent on wasting their money on Formula One. I conducted as much analysis and research as I could come up with. This was to see if we could find any correlation between the sponsorship and business KPIs. We found none. Zero. Nada. Ossi eventually agreed that I should try to negotiate with Mr. Sauber, the owner of the Formula One team, to significantly reduce our way too expensive engagement. Mr. Sauber is a legend in his own right and did not welcome me showing up again and again to negotiate a large reduction. It seemed (to me anyway) that over time, he became more and more relaxed. It soon occurred to me that whenever I left his office, he presumably called Ossi, who most likely told him no substantial change would take place. I became very frustrated and started to openly call out discrepancies and what I deemed a waste of the bank's money. I felt somebody needed to speak up and, since it seemed I was one of the few senior executives with integrity, that had to be me. Three months later Ossi and I agreed that this wasn't working out. One of us would have to leave the bank and he, as CEO, decided it was me. No surprise there! I had been there almost four years and we were finally back to profitability. When I walked out those doors for the last time, I called my wife and said, 'Whatever I do in the future, I will never work with assholes again.'

I'm not saying Ossi was an asshole – although the bank certainly had a culture in which assholes faired amazingly well. In his own way he was an amazing banker and manager. He saved Credit Suisse and, eight years later, UBS and he had Rockstar status among most of the employees. He was a doer that got things done which saved the two largest Swiss banks. Ossi was in that sense a good business leader. But his leadership skills were put to use in a questionable business based on a questionable secrecy law. My issue was really about that and maybe a disappointment that a leader like Ossi did not use his position and skills to significantly change things. As we will see in chapter 8, it took US politicians to force the needed changes. So as good as Ossi was, he fails to qualify as a great business leader as I had a problem with the lack of business ethics in the bank under his leadership. Although that was true for all Swiss banks, it was not ok for me.

# 7.
# FOLLOW YOUR
# PURPOSE

After leaving Credit Suisse, I was quite frustrated and disillusioned with Swiss banking and set out with an aim of improving Swiss banking. It was no easy task but the stupidity I had seen, made me passionate to change the system. In my euphoric state, I decided to set up a strategic management consultancy that would help banks stop the typical mis-use of banking secrecy and actually serve their clients in a real manner. This could be achieved by optimizing long-term profitability rather than short-term. Boy was I naive but, being human, I did not see it at the time. I was used to running businesses and making decisions, and it became clear that I was not the consultant type. I partnered up with a friend, Patrick Koller, who had been a consultant with great firms ever since completing his MBA. In 2004, we started WATC Consulting (What About The Customer) in Zurich. Having been on the executive board of Credit Suisse, I had a vast network and access to most banking CEOs. I was the sales guy and Patrick the intellectual, reflective consultant. It soon became clear to us that most bank CEOs simply did not give a damn. They were all in their 50s, bonuses were excellent, and they had some years left before retirement. Why rock the boat when it might lead to lower profitability in the short-term? My strategy? I learned to sell by being bold and ballsy. I did what McKinsey could not do. I called out CEOs that were stupid. I told them they were wasting their time, told them they lacked ambition and any other insult I could throw at them in the hope of awakening their passion. Most of the time, I was thrown out of their offices; *but* one out of 10 times, I actually faced a CEO who cared, listened, reflected, and became inspired. One of them was Jürgen who ran a very prestigious private bank. He convinced his executive board of the need for change. They were comfortable with the approach to try and treat clients in a way that would make them recommend the bank to their wealthy friends. Now that takes some doing.

In a typical sales pitch, I would advise the CEO to stop all customer research, even if that was the only thing he would do based on meeting me. Most were puzzled as my company, *What About The Customer*, indicated customer research was a key factor. In short, most customer research is a waste. Firstly, 97% of all research does not give real customer insight. They don't tell you what the customer is really willing to pay for and what their choice drivers are. Recall American Express and the real reason for obtaining the card. It was not due to it being widely accepted nor its services – it was mainly to show off to society at large. No typical research study will ever get a customer to admit that. I also questioned customer satisfaction studies. You measure that 85% are satisfied customers. What does that point out? Firstly, it means 15% of your customers are not satisfied and, as the saying goes, an unsatisfied customer will tell 10 acquaintances where a satisfied one tells maybe one to two. Do the math and you will not be surprised that it seems you have a 'declining' business. Secondly, do you know if a satisfied customer purchases more, has more loyalty to your company, etc.? I buy your product *and I expect to be satisfied*. Otherwise, why buy it? But here's the harsh truth. The fact that I'm satisfied does *not* mean I will buy it again or recommend it. It just means I bought a product or service and it worked out as expected. That's it! Have you ever done a price survey? The fact that you have or might need to means you *know* you have a price problem. So, you hire an agency to do a study, but guess what? Your competitors can and probably have done the exact same study so there is *no* competitive advantage. I could go on and on but the end point is that to really succeed, you need to *understand* your customer way beyond what normal customer research is ever capable of doing. The funny thing is, I have most likely spent more money on market research than any other executive simply because I have always pursued fact-based decision making. I analyzed everything so, when I say most market research is a waste of money, I know what I'm talking about.

Back to Jürgen. He bought my arguments and wanted us to bring deeper customer insight to the executive board, in the hopes that this would help them make better, more relevant, and fact-based decisions on the allocation of resources (money and people), leading to increased profitable growth. This is in essence the core task of any management and it was my main goal in setting up WATC. When Patrick and I started WATC, I knew that generating deeper customer insights on actual purchase decision drivers was key for fact-based optimal allocation of resources. We were lucky meeting a psychology professor who explained that psychologists need to understand their patients' conscious as well as subconscious behavior drivers. He explained that by simply having them talk or answer questions, we would only gain conscious behavior drivers and decisions. He then showed us a method that also could uncover unconscious drivers and we were delighted. We decided to bring it to the business world and eventually we had a tool to identify people's *real* choice drivers in buying products. With some modifications we were certain we could deliver a very powerful tool for top management. We had used it in many projects and we used it with Jürgen's clients. Not surprisingly, we found some deep insights that could provoke management. But we pushed Jürgen to go further. Making fact-based decisions based on deep customer insight means you now do the right things. You develop insights for decisions, such as whether to: increase growth, open more branches, advertise more, provide better products, employ more staff, or launch a better digital offering. The insights allow management to decide what is the *right thing* to do to achieve a certain goal. But doing the *things right* is a different game altogether. Most managers and people do what they're required to, but that does not help if they are doing the wrong thing. Combining doing *the right thing* AND *doing it right*, is a power cocktail for success.

Here's an easy example. All restaurants follow the right 'protocol' (more or less). You're taken to your seats and offered a menu. You place your order; they serve your food and provide the bill. So far so good. But *how* they do it differs tremendously. In some restaurants, the owner will come over with a big smile and tell your wife she looks beautiful. They will give you a great table with a lit candle and immediately provide prosecco. He will then explain what the chef bought today on the market and what he recommends. It is now extremely likely that you will take his advice without looking at the menu. Why? Everything has been 'perfect' regarding attention, service to detail, personal recommendation, and so on. If the food turns out on the pricier end, you will justify the reason(s) behind your decision. When leaving the restaurant, your wife will turn around and say, 'Let's come here with Patricia and Peter on Sunday'. But there is a problem – the restaurant is fully booked. The good news? There are plenty of restaurants available. While they follow restaurant protocol, *do the right things*, they may not have the right execution, *doing things right*.

We needed to involve every one of Jürgen's employees in the execution – they needed to understand how it was done *and* why. We established workshops to reach as many employees as possible. We started the workshops by getting participants to talk about their own dismal customer experiences. Many participants went on and on about airlines, restaurants, mobile phone providers, etc. At some point, we asked them, 'While we sit here, criticizing other firms, are some of your clients criticizing your bank?' This was a rhetorical question and, obviously, we knew the answers. We then shared a few deep client insights and asked the cohort to discuss: a) the root problem; b) whether they knew this problem existed; and c) the solutions. This was the 'eureka' moment. A room full of managers would clearly demonstrate they knew: a) exactly what the root cause(s) to the problems were; (b) they knew how long it had been a problem; and (c) they actually knew how they could solve it. This was my cue to ask, 'If this is so, what the hell do you do all day? Why do we have to come here and push you? Why do we have to steer you in the right direction? Why didn't you just do it?' This normally created a bit of a furor where, suddenly, they all agreed they needed to step up and constantly ask themselves: *what about the customer?* They then discussed ways to increase performance for said customers, how to guide the organization to carry out these steps and so on. As one manager said, *'When I go to a Beyoncé concert, not one little thing, not one step, isn't rehearsed a thousand times to have maximum impact on paying concert goers. Nothing is left to coincidence. We should think the same way.'*

We were successful with banks so Patrick and I decided to test our capabilities among the most competitive industries. We decided on mobile providers, car manufactures, and consumer electronics. We soon landed a large German car manufacturer, one of Europe's leading mobile operators, and Philips, a consumer electronics conglomerate. Philips was a particularly interesting case.

When we started with Philips, the CEO had just announced (to the financial analysts) that he would double the growth rate of the firm. One of the key drivers was to become more customer-focused. The plan was to work through every division (TVs, lighting, electric toothbrushes, etc.), and ensure that CEOs and their management team fully understood the need for customer-centric, fact-based decision making. We would do that on the back of a large NPS (Net Promoter Score) initiative that Bain (a consultancy firm) was conducting. This would test the likelihood of customers recommending Philips to others, based on their personal experience *with* Philips. It was a very sensible test and certainly more superior than typical customer satisfaction surveys. If you treat a customer beyond common expectation, they usually end up recommending you – which is always good for business. Bain conducted the survey and we developed and conducted workshops with the executive teams. An excellent example of the outcome can be illustrated by the TV division.

We had a two-day workshop in Singapore with the full executive team from TV. Rather than dwelling on the research done, I asked the management if they knew what day in the week most televisions are purchased. There was no conclusive opinion so I informed them it was Saturday – when people actually have the time. I then asked who purchases televisions, and again, no conclusive opinion. I asked them if they could describe the customer experience in purchasing a television. Not surprising, I received very little coherent feedback. Remember, our objective was to increase growth, and this is done by ensuring all resources, money, and people are allocated to optimal use. To do so, you must understand *how* and *why* people end up purchasing a particular television, and how you can fight for their choice.

I then informed them about the actual 'process': Daddy wakes up Saturday morning and announces to the family that today he will finally buy that new television. The son gets excited and asks if they can watch the space movie in the evening. Naturally, the daughter asks if they can also watch the dragon movie. Daddy assures them both can be done. Mother smiles and decides she will buy popcorn, ensuring a great, fun-filled family evening in front of the new purchase.

Daddy comes home in the early afternoon dragging a huge box with Philips written on it. He unpacks and manages to hang it on the wall. So far so good! The kids are jumping around with excitement. But then, he has to connect the satellite, the Blu-ray system, the Internet and it becomes confusing. He gets slightly irritated. The kids notice and ask, 'Dad, you are going to make it work, right?' The pressure is on and Daddy struggles on, wishing he had bought another television. Mother enters the room and watches the struggling, now swearing, husband and worried kids. 'I should have married Peter, he would have figured it out,' she whispers just loud enough for Daddy to hear it. Just as Daddy is about to explode, he sees an 800-service number. Saved!

He is delighted and calls immediately. He gets a recorded message he interprets as: 'Philips knows most of our customers purchase our televisions on Saturdays, and we know most of you struggle with connections and require our help. However, we have decided not to give a damn so please call us Monday to Friday from eight to six.'

At this point, the CEO stood up, looked at the head of service, and demanded that, as of Saturday, the phone lines would be open again. Not bad, but I was more interested in discussing how Philips had ended up here. How was the decision to suspend the helpline on the weekends made? There were clear statistics that illustrated a vast number of customers purchased their televisions Saturdays and, judging by the research, many struggled with the set-up. The head of the service department explained that the helpline volume was actually lower on Saturdays than any other day in the week. They had therefore decided during the last cost-cutting exercise that keeping the helpline open on Saturdays was not vital, not forgetting it was also the most expensive day to operate the service. What they had obviously missed out on was the *content* of the calls. These calls were from new customers who desperately needed help, and not getting that help pronto made them look like fools in front of their wife and kids. It is never a good thing if your product makes a fool out of your customer, and it's more than likely that the customer will not only *never* purchase a Philips product again but they will probably mention this to their family and friends. The rest of the workshop was then spent on going through customer insight: what drives them to buy Philips, what drives them to buy a competitor's product, and what drives customers to recommend Philips. These insights ultimately helped Philips increase their sales as major decisions were made on how to better allocate resources to cater to this. Management finally understood their key role was *to fight for the customer's choice.*

I used to joke around with my employees at Credit Suisse that if I couldn't make it to the next executive board meeting, they could go instead. They looked skeptical but I told them not to worry, that they would find the meeting so boring that they would actually fall asleep and, even if that did occur, they shouldn't stress about it. Sooner or later, somebody would call out their name and ask what they thought. I advised them to slowly open their eyes, look about very thoughtfully and then state, 'Yes, all good. I just wonder, what about the customer?' I was damn sure that whatever was just discussed had no reflection whatsoever on the customer but, considering the customer could change the entire outcome of the decision, their impact would be solid and just might initiate a discussion about the impact on customers regarding whatever was just decided.

In 2008, four years after starting my consultancy business, the world hit a financial crisis. This was mainly created by the greed and incompetence of the banking industry. Swiss banks suffered many financial blows and even the biggest bank, UBS, had to be saved. More importantly, clients who had trusted their money to the banks had lost a large portion of their assets, and they were not happy. As a consultant to said banks, I realized I had completely failed in improving them and realized I had been naive to think this could happen through being a consultant. In 2009 I was invited as a key speaker at the yearly Private Banking Summit in Zurich. I prepared a strong speech that would suit the very senior executive banking audience. However, just before going on stage, I decided to follow my instinct and scrap my speech. I intended on speaking freely and literally started by saying, *'The worst bankers in the world are sitting in this room.'* I went on to explain that it was not their fault, had nothing to do with stupidity etc. The problem was simply due to Swiss banking secrecy. I argued that it made them lazy and complacent as they did not really have to fight for clients nor provide great solutions. They could simply help clients hide money and save on taxes, or worse, help politicians and civil servants steal money. The room was dead quiet but I was acquainted with most of the top executives and knew they would agree with me in private. However, nobody had stated it so bluntly in an open forum before. After that speech, I decided that rather than being a consultant simply criticizing the current state of banking, I would actually need to show them how to do it. I was energized by my public statements and keener than ever to follow my purpose – to turn banking into an honorable business again. I was not about to give up, and at the same time I also felt I was not going to get a lot of consultancy business from the banks. My speech was very provocative and somewhat insulting – this was alien to the Swiss and would not sit well with managers.

# 8.
# NEVER GIVE UP!

In 2009, at the height of the crisis, I decided to step up and build a customer centric bank targeting entrepreneurs. I didn't know if I could do better than the established banks, but I was certain I would not do worse, and I was passionate about making banking fair for clients. To set up a bank requires CHF 30m in capital – which I did not have. It was clear I needed partners and that dictated our new concepts: gather successful entrepreneurs that hold no love for traditional banks, and offer them part-ownership in their own bank! Getting the right people, the ones who would deposit most of their wealth at the bank, would make the bank successful. However, I felt that merely managing assets is no value-add. Asset management is basically a commodity with very little value-add for most clients. Given that the target group were entrepreneurs, their excitement was not based on making another 4–7% on the stock market but on their businesses and potential deals. The asset management department would focus on keeping their money safe i.e. not losing it. That, of course, made for very conservative asset management, which in my view makes a lot of sense. I am always astonished when business people, capable of making vast fortunes, are obsessed with returns on their hard-earned money. In fact, they're so obsessed they hand that responsibility to young bankers that have *zero* clue. What's worse, these young bankers do not know they have no clue! They are conventionally trained, receive a great deal of financial information, and basically think they are Soros. One of my close friends who is quite wealthy (and who you will meet later in the book) usually asks them, 'If you're so smart, why aren't you rich?' Well, perhaps they aren't so smart. One thing was certain – they were definitely trying to get rich, and not by investing your money smartly, but by investing them in high fee generating products. That way they received big bonuses without doing anything smart for the client and, truth be told, it was (and is) a totally misaligned business model. Unfortunately, just because a client knows how to build a successful business, does not mean he or she understand anything about investing and banking.

In my view, once you accept the responsibility of managing other people's money, it is your job to keep it safe. I have seen reputable banks fold, so my bank needed to do better. I decided the bank's capital, all CHF 30m, would be placed in the Swiss National Bank rather than used as bank capital to maximize profit. That said, the bank would be 'safe', although many people told me I would miss out on the 'essence' of banking through this passive approach. I saw it differently and didn't see why hardworking entrepreneurs (who made enough money anyway) needed to risk their money in the markets or with an undercapitalized bank. Who knows, they might need it one day. The real value-add my bank presented was that the entrepreneurs could use the bank as their business platform. This meant the bank supported their business endeavors and also engaged in club deals. Take an entrepreneur from Brazil with resources, put him or her together with a German technology entrepreneur and a Chinese business entrepreneur with access to the Chinese market, and you're taking business to a whole new level! Having a Swiss bank as the trusted platform mitigates some of the larger trust issues. In short, we would help our clients develop their business through a global network and club deals, while keeping their hard-earned money safe for a rainy day or a great business opportunity. In addition, our clients earned profits as shareholders. It goes without saying that stating one owns a Swiss bank impresses even the most successful industry titan as well as the pretty girl in the bar. I had a differentiated, highly relevant proposition for a clear target group and just needed to meet that target group in order to convince them.

I decided to travel around the world to select my partners/clients. It was an immensely interesting experience meeting people from a great many countries and industries. I also experienced all manner of crooks, which wasn't surprising seeing as word slipped out that I was setting up a Swiss bank and offering partial ownership. I could write a book on the people I met, and I'm sure I feature on multiple secret service records for having met the wrong kind of people. The bad news is you actually have to meet people before you can really judge them. The good news is that when you finally do meet them, it does not take long to figure out their true motives and source of wealth. You have to go through well prepared documents from their (Swiss) lawyers, who are quite happy to support such individuals with dubious businesses. It is truly amazing that Switzerland still maintains that 'clean reputation' around the world. The harsh truth is Switzerland has indeed helped most crooks (local and global) hide money, starting with the Nazis. And then, there is the kicker: Switzerland proudly stating they are neutral... as if that is a virtue. I have a special quote for them from Dante, 'The darkest places in hell are reserved for those who maintain their neutrality in times of moral crisis.' You're wondering why I decided on Switzerland as a basis for my banking endeavor, seeing as I reserve a great deal of criticism for their operating procedures. Despite the dodgy banking model, Switzerland is still seen as a great place to keep one's money: it is a democratic county with a stable economy, strong currency, and a favorite travel destination.

Eventually, through the passion and dedicated effort of someone who became my closest partner and friend, Antonio, we had a group of great visionaries who would provide the required capital. That turned out to be the easy part. The hard bit was obtaining a banking license. This was at the same time as UBS was saved by the Government, and in an economic downturn there was increased pressure on banking secrecy. Obviously, politicians in many countries, particularly in

Europe and the US, found it very unfair that, while their countries were in crisis, their wealthy citizens avoided paying taxes by hiding money in Switzerland. A wave of criticism concerning Swiss banking secrecy gained momentum, and it was the bold moves of the US that changed the game. The US requested, from UBS initially and all Swiss banks eventually, that they inform them of their US clients. Obviously, this goes against the Swiss banking secrecy concept but, by pushing hard and buying some 'stolen' CDs containing client names, the US threatened to close out the banks from the dollar system. That was in addition to the arrest of a few Swiss bankers, so Swiss banks had no choice and started cooperating, some more willingly than others. Of course, we still had greedy Swiss bankers who thought they could simply transfer clients to a branch in another jurisdiction. Naive thinking, of course, and this eventually caught up with them, resulting in huge fines, bank closures, and – for some – jail. The Swiss banking model, also known as helping people cheat in taxes, was coming to a quick end – finally. You can choose your taxes by choosing where to live but, wherever you chose to live, good citizenship requires you to pay taxes. If you skirt them, it is always the little man that loses out, the one that cannot afford the tax experts, lawyers, and structures. All this ultimately furthers unequal wealth distribution – which history has proven to be a bad idea.

The Swiss banking regulator, FINMA, was in the middle of it. Although Switzerland's largest bank had just been saved, many banks were facing the death scenario. I walk in to the regulator, saying I want to create a new bank with a new business model. Now remember, regulators are in essence state employees. Instead of listing a long cascade of silly communication and experiences, everything basically came down to this: FINMA did not appreciate my unique approach with safety, conservative asset management, and merchant banking for the clients. They also did not appreciate a broader ownership circle of wealthy individuals so I faced two major obstacles. After two years of trying to convince them, FINMA (directly) suggested that I simply apply for a license to run a normal private bank. After seeing my business plan, they even suggested I raise client fees. What?! The Swiss private banking model was dead, there were 320 private banks with most struggling, and they want me to start down that road? Really?! I was at a loss trying to understand this. Apparently, regulators are not to be understood, merely followed. It was extremely frustrating but that was just the beginning. After years of providing information and discussion, I learned that the last thing they wanted was a new bank. They actually wanted less banks and was hoping for a consolidation. I understood they would do anything to avoid a new bank *but* that they could not tell me this. If they wrote that in a letter, I could make a case where I could prove I lived up to all set standards, obligations, and procedures. They kept on asking for more information and documentation in the hopes I would get tired or run out of money. They didn't realize I was on a mission, but I clearly had to change gears. In the end, we agreed I would acquire an existing bank, a normal private bank with recurring revenue where I could do my intended business at the same time.

Antonio and I set out to buy a bank. By now, we had spent millions of Swiss Francs and wasted a few years. The Swiss banking environment changed from bad to worse so our passion to not only 'set things right' but to succeed grew. Initially, we looked at 10 banks in Zurich but they were garbage. No business model, even worse management, and of course, undercapitalized. In the end, we found a bank in Lugano, Switzerland, where we ended up buying 70% with our circle of partners/clients. We shortened the FINMA approval process by ensuring only myself and a colleague who would run compliance would be qualified shareholders. We were seen as people qualified to run a bank, and therefore allowed to own more than 10% of it. The rest of the shareholders owned just under 5% and that saved us years of approval harassment.

The bank was making a small loss when we bought it, but we turned this around and ran a profitable bank. We did make one major mistake through. The two original founders, who FINMA insisted keep 25%, turned out to be managers, not leaders. They worked hard to help us buy the bank and managed part of the FINMA approval. They toasted partnership and friendship as we closed the deal but from day one it became clear that they were afraid of the new vision and strategy. Actually, the word 'new' is misleading as they had no vision or strategy when we bought them. The bank was small, unprofitable, and had unsatisfied shareholders that wanted to sell. As a leader you should discuss strategy; you can agree or disagree on strategy but to omit strategic discussion altogether was not what I had in mind, and exactly what they tried to do. I set up weekly partner meetings with both and to my amazement they had nothing to share. No ideas, no suggestions – they were a blank page. They were proud to dig deep into compliance issues and ensure the bank avoided new, ground breaking strategies as anything new seemed risky to them. One of the bank managers, was a highly intelligent person. While his intelligence was something to note, he lacked vision, was incapable of making any strategic reflections, and 'managed' people to fear him. It became a daily struggle to deal with him as a partner. I soon learned the staff were terrified of him and did anything he asked without question. The two managers were busy all day, micromanaging every little detail while avoiding the bigger picture. No wonder they had failed to build a successful bank. Through using an intimidating management style, the bank could not boast about having the best or smartest employees as such people would never succumb to this style. I spent a lot of time talking to the employees, trying to understand what went on. It seems they were not allowed to discuss such issues yet, at the same time, they instilled hope in me. I was keen to unlock the potential of the bank, but every initiative or new client that wanted something slightly different from the standard offer was blocked. Nevertheless, we brought in many new clients and increased the asset base fivefold. I spent most of my time trying to nurture real business deals to and from our entrepreneurial clients, and all in all we built a profitable bank in the span of a few years.

I was still unhappy about the bank being unable to function at its full potential. It was not just the two managers holding us back but the regulator trying to manage in the aftermath of the financial crisis. They wanted to guarantee that this crisis was a one-off, never-to-be-repeated scenario and that basically killed the fun of running the bank as well as our ability to provide clients with great solutions. Everything was compromised and, while compromise can be important in some situations, I felt I had compromised my vision for far too long. I decided to leave the bank and sell my shares. After six long years and a great deal of money, we had built a profitable bank but were fatally tackled by managers (my 'partners') and civil servants (the regulator). We had amazing people involved and taking interest, visionary leaders that would run the bank, great clients that were an asset in itself, potential board members that could choose to sit on any board they wanted etc.; but the regulator insisted on the 'managers' having the majority of the power and there was nothing we could do against that.

My journey had taken me from fighting at Credit Suisse, then advising banks on strategy, to finally having my own bank. I had spent almost 15 years pursuing my passion, trying to make the banking industry a value-adding honorable business again. In the end the system was too strong, too well established, and had no incentives to change, financially or otherwise. The decision to direct my energy elsewhere was not easy but it was the right one. Looking at the banking industry today, stuffed with regulators and compliance issues, it's a miserable business to be in. I became one of those who left the banking world for good, and I am truly convinced that, since the crisis, the smartest people in banking (all of those who know how to add value, and get things done, or service clients well) have left banking to start their own businesses, or work in fintech, or another interesting field. Smart people don't have room to maneuver in a highly regulated, compliance-oriented business-like banking with little to offer the clients. I had learned a great deal and had an amazing time in terms of the people I met. While I was glad that the bank had improved significantly, it was frustrating to know that it could have been so much more. I never gave up, until giving up was the only right thing to do; it sometimes is.

# 9.
# VENTURE CAPITAL
# AND START-UPS

During my banking endeavor, the first person I approached as a client was one of Europe's extremely successful entrepreneurs, Dr. Cornelius Börsch ('Conny'). I mentioned him earlier as the man rhetorically asking bankers, 'If you're so smart, why aren't you rich?' Conny had not only built two massive technology businesses but he had successfully exited at a young age, becoming very wealthy and famous. His real passion though was investing in internet businesses and helping young entrepreneurs succeed. This passion had made him Europe's most active business angel, which led to many wealthy people wanting to co-invest with him. In 2005, he transformed his family office, then managed by a smart young man, Daniel, into an investment company called Mountain Partners. When I asked Conny to join my bank, he had a portfolio of 50 start-ups – all needing capital, or ready for merger, or full exit – ideal for a merchant bank. He was the ideal potential business partner for my bank and, after listening to my idea, he stated that he was in and offered to help any way he could. When it became obvious that FINMA was making us jump through numerous hoops and it was taking much longer than anticipated to get started, he asked me to join him as a partner in Mountain Partners. Obviously, I could not jump ship but as he was my most important client in the bank (potentially), I offered to help as much as I could. I started accompanying him on his business trips around the world and paid attention to his interaction with people. I was deeply impressed by his raw enthusiasm for helping young people become entrepreneurs and create successful digital businesses. Though it was for profit, he was proud of his personal input in the field of job creation and the impact he had. I was also deeply impressed by his network. Whichever country we visited, we always met with leading families or industrialists, several of whom decided to invest with Mountain Partners.

Conny's vast global network partly originated from the years when he was politically engaged. He had come across a young man who wanted to form a new party in Germany, and Conny had decided to help him, eventually providing and raising most of the campaign financing. Eventually the young politician, Guido Westerwelle, became the Vice-Chancellor of Germany and the Foreign Minister. Conny became his party's senior advisor. On our trips, Conny would provide endlessly entertaining stories about travelling to countries like Syria and being chauffeured around in a tank with the German vice-chancellor, or reminding him on a plane to Saudi Arabia that gays can be executed there. The vice-chancellor was gay so it was solid advice.

Conny and I got to appreciate each other and soon realized that we had very complementary skills: he was a true entrepreneurial visionary leader and I knew how to build institutional businesses and internationalize them. Some years later, after selling my shares in the bank, Conny again invited me to join him. I bought into the company and became Conny and Daniel's partner. Before I jumped on board, we finalized the company's vision. From what I saw, venture capital was totally different from any other asset class I had ever seen. In a nutshell, if you're very smart you can figure out how to invest in stocks, bonds, real estate, and maybe even private equity. That same intelligence will get you almost nothing in the world of venture capital. Nine out of 10 start-ups eventually fail, and the one that succeeds might not give your money back tenfold. Most investors, including

VC funds, actually lose money. At the time, Conny and Daniel had 15 years of venture capital investing experience and, may I say, had made every mistake possible! There was a huge 'knowledge base' that could be utilized to make it work and institutionalize it at the same time. Don't get me wrong, they had success but with their experience and effort they could have more going forward. We set out to make Mountain Partners an early stage venture capital firm with a risk management approach, reducing the three major risks start-ups face: execution, business model, and financing. We started focusing on building companies from scratch rather than just investing. Why? Because every entrepreneur starting a business seems to repeat the same mistakes as all predecessors. We could help avoid those mistakes if we were in from day one and thereby reduce the execution risk.

Typically, a management team will come to you with a great idea. Most people will look at the idea and see the business plan states that by capturing just 0.5% of the market the business will break even in year 3 or 4, and it will later be worth close to one billion. That's not going to happen in 9,999 out of 10,000 cases. The problem is we always pay attention to that lone case and therefore believe it is possible. Forget the 0.5% of the market, go out and get the first two paying customers, and forget about breaking even in year 3 or 4 – you're actually looking at year 7 to 10! Forget the unicorn valuation; what's wrong with just building a solid, cash flow positive business? Another thing – management teams are often school buddies. That's great as far as longevity of your friendships go but that does not mean they are the right management team for a certain idea. We were provocative in our approach, 'So you have a great idea – who cares?!' An idea is not worth anything without the right team behind its execution. It all comes down to this: if they want our money, they will have to agree to a management team *we believe* have the right experience. And that included experience in start-ups and the industry they play in. Giving people money – who have never launched a start-up, in an industry they have never worked in, with a business model that has not been done before – is, in 999 out of 1,000 cases, simply stupid. Such investments fail; it's why most people have lost money in start-ups and concluded that investing in start-ups does not work.

Would you let a normal doctor without surgical experience, operate on your knee? Exactly. Furthermore, they must agree to be mentored by serial entrepreneurs, at our offices, for the first two years, on a daily basis. With that approach to minimizing the execution risk, we avoided common mistakes and our success rate of our businesses spiraled upwards of 80%, not the more common 10%. As we provided the seed capital in exchange for 50% of the business, the returns were quite interesting. Management received the remaining 50%. It was important they felt, as owners, that it was *their* business and required *their* effort when it came to solving problems – and there are always numerous problems in the first few years.

After discovering that we were capable of building successful businesses from scratch, we decided to build a global factory, German style. We were not manufacturing Mercedes automobiles but producing start-ups. We entered several countries in South America, Asia, and the Middle-East. Countries that, as yet, had no start-up ecosystem and desperately needed to create jobs for their younger generations. These were countries with large populations, low salaries, but great Internet and mobile penetration. In 2015, my family and I travelled to Africa and I recall the Masai tribesman dressed in traditional garb. I gathered he was a goat herder and saw he held a shepherd's staff in one hand. What do you think was in the other? A smart phone. How amazing is that? These countries still lacked many of the basic digital business models that were already proven in other countries, so we decided to clone business models already proven in another country, rather than investing in a brand-new idea. With the proven models, we knew the economics, the key KPIs to watch, and the skills required by the management team, thereby reducing the business model risk. We had already reduced the execution risk through our unique approach to start-ups, and all that was left was the financing risk. Say we suddenly had 10 Mexican start-ups that each need two million. That's 20 million which we might not have and cannot raise in London. One of the greatest factors contributing to the failure of start-ups is the drying up of finances. Why? The founders promise to break even in year three or four but fail, investors get disappointed and lose faith. They pull out and the start-up now has to raise money without current investors participating. It's a hard sell and most firms fail. However, if management gets the financing, support, and time they need they can eventually create a successful business. You might start out with a B2C business model but, through experience and persistence, you learn that you must adapt to a B2B business model to make it successful. The need for ongoing financing, as long as you believe in the business and the team, is crucial for getting it right. We therefore joined up with local business families to provide the needed local growth capital for our start-ups. We ended up building a global start-up 'factory' that reduced risks in the business model, execution, and financing – it worked out very well and was a lot of fun.

Over the next five years, we grew the numbers of firms from 50 to 150 and Mountain Partners value went up by three times. We felt we had the experience and success to confirm that early stage venture capital can work. We weren't necessarily smarter than others; we turned down many businesses that later proved to be unicorns, and we exited some of our most successful businesses too early (there was a reason why someone wanted to buy it), and we have seen 50 businesses fail – businesses we thought would be unicorns. Understanding the reasons behind those failures was our biggest asset. Intelligence alone won't give you a solid foundation for investing successfully in venture capital – those painful loses teach you to be successful, if you're savvy enough to learn from them!

This long and winding process was mainly driven by Conny's enthusiasm and strong beliefs. He invested his own money when needed, convinced important strategic partners, ensured an on-going opportunistic and entrepreneurial approach, even as we institutionalized the business. Many told us we were wrong, that it does not work and so forth, but Conny didn't listen. Furthermore, Conny's leadership ensured we attracted great talents, although we paid lower than average compensation compared to everybody else. We attracted people who saw the vision and purpose, and who wanted to be part of the success. We weren't interested in individuals who were hunting out the highest salaries. Conny was a true leader and, may I say, a terrible daily manager. He knew this though and refrained from poking around the daily business, deciding to trust the doings to the experts. He is a visionary with true passion and one of the earliest leaders in this global trend. Because of this, he became entrepreneur of the year, business angel of the year, an accredited investor with the European Investment Bank, invested in over 250 start-ups, created more than 10,000 jobs, and, of course, made some good money on the way.

Many of the large corporations, like telecoms, media firms, insurance and banks have or are in the process of transforming their business to a digital model, and they have all failed. There are no real examples of a major corporation that actually succeeded in transforming into a *leading* digital business. Why? Because they take a managerial approach, relying on managers to do it all, and it fails every single time. For some God-awful reason, they keep doing it! That said, this was a great opportunity for Mountain as we could offer the perfect partnership for these corporations.

Conny, being the visionary leader he is, is not married to any set idea. Although we were in love with the company building approach, we soon realized it required a great deal of capital to keep backing the best companies. This is a long-term game where returns materialize after seven to 10 years. When that realization hit us, Conny wanted us to adapt to investors' expectations: shorter investing period and more liquidity. We therefore started adding more VC asset management by offering funds, listed VC vehicles, and co-investment opportunities, all to ensure we could cater to, and raise enough money from investors, for all the great investment opportunities we came across. Conny will be at it for another 15 to 20 years, working his usual 80-hour week, and it is rewarding to be part of this.

In July 2017, Conny and I met one of the founders of a Blockchain firm who asked us to invest. We heard a story that was too good to be true, and it came hand in hand with a valuation that was 50 times higher than any we would consider. Being experienced in fantasy business ideas, unrealistic expectations, and ridiculous evaluations, it was a relatively short meeting that ended in a firm no from our side. But due to the incredible story, Conny and I decided that I would stay in touch with the firm and follow their progress. So, I did…

# 10.
# WORK ON SOMETHING WITH IMMENSE POTENTIAL

I have always been passionate about any job or task I committed myself to. I was passionate about eliminating cash, and making insurance 'customer friendly'. I was passionate about people investing for their retirement, and enabling people to manage their own money, successfully. I was passionate about turning Swiss banking around, where it had the chance to become an honorable business again. I was passionate about helping start-ups and creating entrepreneurs. But, in all honesty, I had spent most of my life helping wealthy people to become wealthier, and that really didn't change the world for the better. When I was offered the opportunity to help change the world for the better using Blockchain, it was a no-brainer. It took me a long time to understand Blockchain technology, and even longer to fully capture its potential capabilities for solving some of the world's most pressing issues. Once I did, I was hooked.

The Blockchain firm's founders (they are still operating under the radar so no names will be mentioned) claimed that they would build a new Blockchain platform, a next-generation Internet – the Internet of value, not just information. They claimed that they had solved the constraints of Blockchain technology to finally make it enterprise ready on a grand scale. They claimed that with their Blockchain, they could build a trusted society where people would own their data and identities (essentially killing off Google, Facebook, and the rest) and secure people's privacy. The digitalization of identities, would also allow inclusion of the one billion people that have no official identity, and are therefore closed off from not just basic services but also from participating in any economic activity. They further claimed that their platform could digitalize virtually every possible asset, while adhering to local rules and regulations, and thereby build a new economy on a grand scale of access and liquidity of illiquid assets , benefiting all people in the world – rich and poor. They claimed that the global operating platform they were building would allow governments and institutions to build ground-breaking applications with which some of the world's most pressing problems could be solved, such as climate change, inequality by eradicating corruption, and tax fraud. I had watched the *The Great Hack*, a documentary illustrating how personal data was used by Cambridge Analytica to manipulate voters, among others, and influence election outcomes in several countries, including in the US presidential race in 2016. I wondered whether we had finally entered the age where democracy had an expiration date but now Blockchain gave me hope. Obviously, their claims were huge but if they could pull it off, they could be building the most amazing company the world have ever seen. I have seen many pitches in my lifetime but none that came anywhere close to the level of arrogance, ambition, and vision of this one. I was intrigued and they had my attention.

There were four founders, but they didn't get along very well so I initially met up with two of them. One was a highly intelligent and thoroughly impressive computer scientist who was also a serial entrepreneur. The other was a salesman but like nothing I'd ever seen. He pitched their project, and though the firm hadn't developed their platform or acquire a single customer, he offered me the opportunity to invest at a $500m valuation. His key argument for the valuation was that a well-known billionaire was investing quite a chunk at the same valuation based on the advice of his advisor, a former investment banker from an American highly regarded bank. That poor guy (a funny expression for a man born a billionaire) did simply not have the experience to judge the valuation and, for whatever reason, his advisor who should have known much better, must have supported the valuation. Go figure… I offered to invest at a valuation of $15m, which was rejected flat out. I didn't mind because I didn't know whether the business could support even that valuation. Despite my offer, the two founders stayed in touch and provided more insight to the technology and its potential applications for governments, institutions, and businesses. The more I learned, the more excited I became.

It took another year for me to meet the main brain behind it all (let's call him Peter). Peter is a mathematical and cryptography genius, par excellence, and one of the smartest people I have ever met. He chattered on endlessly, excitedly about Blockchain's ability to change the world and why all current players, IBM and Ethereum included, would fail with their technologies. Peter was also a serial entrepreneur and had built a number of businesses, one of which was acquired by a leading Silicon Valley firm, giving them a key technological advantage. He had also built payment systems and assisted new challenger banks to establish themselves in the digital and crypto space. It took a year to meet Peter because the man was overwhelmed trying to get along with the other founders. Instead, he had settled on creating solutions with his own team: solutions that would run on the Blockchain platform. It was Peter who brought the pitch to life, and he had endless ideas on how to make a success of it. It was clear that I had finally met the man behind the vision of the firm. Shortly after meeting Peter, the company realized that they would need another year to develop the platform. This was a huge problem as they were running out of funds. Peter soon asked for a private meeting that ended up becoming the start of my involvement in the firm. He informed me that he was the largest shareholder and wanted to take over as CEO, but he wanted and needed my help. As I mentioned before, Peter is quite smart with numerous talents, one of which is knowing his own limitations. He was not a natural-born CEO but realized that by taking on the position temporarily, he could get the company back on course and make it attractive for investors. I was delighted to be asked, delighted to finally get involved, and delighted at the opportunity to work with him. I committed myself wholeheartedly and we spent the next year making a full turnaround.

At the time of writing, the company has almost finished building the platform and have multiple use cases ready for execution. Our billionaire invested once again, and this gave the opportunity to correct the previous 'situation' that had been unfair to him. This proved a smart move as he since has been a tremendous source of support to the business. The firm is set to change the world! Being a realist, I know numerous problems can crop up, but we are finally on the map, and who knows, we might be the next Microsoft – or we might go bankrupt as we are still a start-up... Success is never linear, and the firm (as with most other successful start-ups) had to overcome a dysfunctional founding team, massive delays in programming, overspending, and a ridiculously high valuation. On the plus side, it proved the importance of having a strong investor who believed enough in the business to stick with it through thick and thin. As long as such investors do not interfere in the operation of the business, it is a blessing. I have seen numerous business go down when investors suddenly believe they know better, or they insist on unqualified advisors representing them either on the board or in management. Such moves demotivate or even chase the founders away and that is always the beginning of the end.

Peter had assembled an amazing tech team dedicated to constructing what we hope will become a global leader in Blockchain technology. We are in sync, speak up to five times a day and make every decision together. I have become more involved than what I had initially signed up for but love every minute of it!

One of the use cases the firm is in the process of launching is a major carbon credit initiative with strategic partners: the aim is to make a solid contribution toward reducing the climate crisis. Our partners include governments, major institutions, and businesses who believe we can better incentivize, measure, and produce carbon absorbing activities, and capture this in digital certificates that eventually can be traded, all on Blockchain. This will allow a globally transparent, incorruptible carbon credit system through which governments and businesses can finally pursue *true* carbon neutrality.

I am at last involved in something that can effect real positive change for the world, and it feels great! I will highlight all the possibilities Blockchain provides for a better world in chapter 20. I wish I had gotten involved in something like this much earlier in my life but it is never too late.

# 11.
# BE AN ENTREPRENEUR

Looking back, I wish I had become involved in the entrepreneurial world much earlier. Knowing what I know today, I wasted too much time and effort fighting corporate politics with incompetent managers. In the entrepreneurial world, you mainly deal with leaders or at least with people who have a purpose and a passion. These people aren't focused on their next pay check and not afraid of making mistakes. They're people who are willing to work long hours, without vacation to realize their mission. Individuals who stand up for their beliefs and keep moving forward when everybody else tells them to quit. Having started two firms myself and being partner in two others, I can tell you that it's bloody hard but rewarding (although not always in financial terms). Entrepreneurs who do it for the money often fail. Those who follow their passion typically do succeed at some point, but it's a long, hard journey which usually affects marriages or relationships negatively. It's not for everyone, and I personally believe you either have it or you don't. You can't take this path whimsically with a 'Hey, I want to be an entrepreneur!' You need purpose and passion you would be willing to die for (almost), anything less and you will certainly fail.

In the following chapters, I describe two famous entrepreneurs who both became two of the richest men in the world. They worked extremely hard for their success and, upon reaching that, continued working long hours rather than enjoying what they had created. The 500 or so (successful) entrepreneurs I have met through banking and the Mountain Partners endeavor had the same traits. They were smart enough to be able to have had successful corporate careers and easy lives (I believe corporate careers are easy if you are willing to play the necessary politics), but chose not to go down that route. I believe they simply felt they were doing what was necessary and there was no acceptable alternative. I'm well known for not being a fan of business dinners and felt I wasted too much time during my corporate career dining with high ranking but totally uninteresting managers. Interestingly, I would happily go to dinner with an entrepreneur at any time. The majority of people that inspired me were entrepreneurs and, in fact, entrepreneurs have the biggest impact.

If you are a young soul reading this and feel an inexplicable need to *be that change*, quit your job tomorrow and find something you burn for, something fun and inspirational with meaning, and (hopefully) a positive impact. Don't follow the crowd only to end up not giving a damn. Follow your passion and be a leader!

# PART II

## GREAT LEADERS

# 12.
# CAN YOU LEARN GREAT LEADERSHIP SKILLS?

In the first part, I have described my experiences and opinions on leaders and managers, clearly praising the former over the latter. Why am I so obsessed with leaders? Frankly, we need them. The world needs them. Think about it. Most people, causes, and opportunities need leaders and strong leadership. Most achievements, positive or negative, have only been realized due to a strong leader. Bill Gates created Microsoft and believed every home should have a computer. Rockefeller led the oil revolution in producing and transporting oil. Henry Ford led the car industry, making cars the average middle-class person could afford. Ernesto 'Che' Guevara, after seeing the sorry state of people in every county he travelled through in South America, led the Cuban revolution. J.P Morgan was a leader, financially enabling the industrial revolution and inspiring the creation of the National Bank. Alexander the Great was a military leader that ended up creating one of the greatest empires in world history. Andrew Carnegie led the US to become the number one steel-producing nation through management efficiency. Ray Kroc industrialized the world, for worse, to eat fast, convenient (and unhealthy) food through his McDonald's burger chain. Kiichiro Toyoda built the world's largest automaker, Toyota. Winston Churchill led the campaign that ended Hitler. Speaking of which, Adolf Hitler displayed leadership skills and how destructive they can be when embedded with the wrong ideals. Julius

Caesar is said to have been a genius leader who played a critical role in the rise of the Roman Empire. Mao Zedong, aka Chairman Mao, drove out imperialism and laid the foundations for China to become a Super Power. Martin Luther King Jr. led the non-violent civil rights movement, fighting for racial equality. Nelson Mandela was the leader and the face of the Anti-Apartheid movement in South Africa and became its first democratically elected President. Mahatma Gandhi led India against the tyrannical rule of the British Empire.

These are just a few of the well-known leaders the world has seen. Imagine if they had not existed. Each of them changed and shaped the world in their own way, most for the better, some for the worse. Without the great leaders, we would have achieved less and our lives would have been very different, most likely worse (like we all would speak German). We need leaders, as the world highly depends on them. But what makes a great leader and will there always be great leaders?

On a trip through Bhutan, accompanied by a very interesting, spiritual crowd, I was introduced to the idea of Human Design. The Human Design System, invented, projected to, or derived by (depending on your beliefs) Ra Uru Hu (real name Alan Robert Krakower), says that each human is uniquely designed with a specific purpose to fulfil during their time on earth. It is said to be a tool based on old sciences, such as Kabbala astrology and I Ching, combined in new ways and connected to new knowledge within Quantum Physics and genetics. It stampedes astrology and takes the idea much further. I personally don't believe in astrology (one of my favorite books is *Debunked* by Georges Charpak and Henri Broch in which science debunks astrology, among others things). It is not important whether we believe in it or not. The real question is this: is there something that can push our thinking further? For the moment, let's entertain the idea that there is 'something' out there guaranteeing our uniqueness. Human Design offers a theory and I was open to the group leader, Yana, explaining the idea in greater detail. She explained it in broad terms but, more importantly, she had prepared a Human Design chart for each person in our little group. She went on for hours explaining who we are, what our role is, etc. When she came to explain me, I was somewhat flabbergasted by what I heard. It was a spot-on insightful and revealing explanation of my person and my life. Being somewhat surprised by this accurate description, I waited until she had finished with all eight people and, before anyone commented, asked everyone to tell me on a scale from one to ten how accurate they felt the description of them was. Almost all said a clear 10 with few saying nine. While I don't believe in the story of Ra Uru Hu, there was something logical to what I learned.

Let's dive into the 'logical' part of my experience which is relevant to this book. One of the many things Human Design does is to describe what each individual's purpose is on earth. Human Design splits us into four main categories, and stipulates that each person is born into one of these categories:

**Generators:** These are people who build things, do things, execute things. They will respond to what is given to them or asked of them. They don't take initiative but follow instructions. It is said they compose roughly 70% of the population at any given time. Makes sense, right? Someone has to harvest the fields, build the factories, and manufacture products etc.

**Manifestors**: These are individuals who take the initiative. They play an important role as someone must take the initiative before the generators can build or execute. They seek to communicate their ideas and initiatives clearly, thereby inspiring others to follow.

**Projectors:** This group passively waits to be recognized, and when recognized and invited to participate, are happy to help guide. They do not take initiative on their own but are happy to guide others.

**Reflectors:** These are the ones that take time to reflect and decide, and they are said to be the judges of humanity and, I assume, ideas. Through their reflections, they challenge what is being done, sometimes destroying, other times improving.

Now, let's leave the spiritual, magical dimension behind and get back to business. What does this mean? It could mean that some people are born to be leaders. It seems obvious that the Manifestors, who initiate change, are the leaders. Projectors are the managers, Generators the workers, and Reflectors would be people like professors, researchers, philosophers etc. This last group is said to compose less than 1% of the population. Workers, as already said, make up around 70%, Projectors make up 22%, and Manifestors make up the rest. There is great logic in understanding that we all serve different key roles that make society function and progress. Imagine if humanity composed of leaders alone? I'm sure you have attended a meeting or two where a few people perceived themselves to be the leaders in charge. The result is likely an unproductive meeting, a possible fight among the egos, and a few huffy attitudes. What if everyone turned out to be from the Reflectors category? That wouldn't work either. So, I subscribe to the likely fact that some people are natural born leaders, others are not, and this ensures that our society keeps progressing.

It must be said that we depend equally on the other types, and though I questioned the validity of managers (Projectors) in the first part of the book, after having read the full description of Projectors, I put this down to the fact that most managers actually try to take the initiative, which is outside their core competencies (according to Human Design). In large organizations, Projectors (managers) are trying to expand their role beyond the role 'assigned' to them at birth. This fits pretty well because there are many good managers out there. It's the ones with huge egos, the ones that want to do more than they're capable of or the ones that have been promoted one time too many (called the Peter principle) that are the problem. Anyway, let's leave my scrutiny of managers and get back to leaders.

The world is dependent on leaders and it is highly likely that we have always had them among us, and always will. A few key questions pop up: Are there potential leaders, people born into leadership? Can we foster leaders? What are the core leadership skills and traits, and can people choose to take on the mantle of leadership? To answer these questions, it's important to better understand leaders and leadership by looking into some of the greats.

# 13.
# THE WORLD'S GREAT LEADERS

Who are great leaders? Well, if you google 'great leaders' you get many different answers. There also seems to be a separation between business leaders and leaders within a non-business, mostly political cause. That's helpful and I will use the same distinction. If we look at Ranker's 'The Most Important Leaders in World History' list, the result is a crowd ranking rather than one person's view. This is both good and bad. It's bad because it fast becomes clear that the term Leader is applied very broadly, and without a proper definition. On the other hand, it represents a broader perception. But then, looking at the names on the list (fifty in total) I realized that many of the people listed are so far off the mark of what I expect in great leadership. Ranked number 23rd is Jesus Christ and Muhammad comes in at 39th place. This makes me think. There are no first-hand accounts of these people's deeds. Although the Quran was written relatively shortly after Muhammad's death, the Bible was written hundreds of years later based on stories passed from generation to generation. And although they still today have a huge following, it is not factually clear what net positive impact they have had on the world. Are the ten commandments basic human attributes or do we not kill each other, for example, because we were told by a god not to do so? And haven't more people in the world been killed in these figures' names than for any other cause? This is a long and difficult discussion which is proven by the fact that there is a long online debate following the list, and the debate is mainly focused on exactly these two figures. The debate is at a very low level by passionate followers of either of these two figures. Anyway, I will decide to omit them in my consideration for 'great leaders' and any similar figures (like Moses, ranked 27th). The list also contains people that led by brutal violence, often to conquer what is not rightfully theirs. I have decided to also omit these kinds of leaders, which then also removes Stalin and Hitler, from my further consideration. Then ranked number 12th is Donald J. Trump. Well, whatever we think of Trump, it's still too early to rate him on his policies, history will have to do so at a later date. One thing that clearly disqualifies him in my eyes? Under his presidency, America seems more divided than ever. I happen to believe that the only way anything good can be achieved under democracy is to have strong leadership that can unite interests. A *great leader* must seek to unite rather than divide so Trump is definitely out for that, and endless other reasons. A unique thought strikes me here: I have mentioned both Trump and Jesus. If there were no recordings of Trump, no videos, no first-hand accounts of his deeds and behavior, how would *The Donald* be reflected on in a few hundred years when someone decided to write a book about him? His followers have shown tremendous loyalty and willingness to close their eyes to his negative traits, so they would tell their offspring that he is amazing, and their offspring would probably relate that he was a supreme being etc. No doubt a few hundred years down the line, he would be described as though he could 'walk' on water. For those who see him as a liar, narcissist, and demagogue, he would (a few hundred years later) be described as a devil. That's just an interesting thought on which I will draw no conclusions…

Rather than go through the entire list where I disqualify people based on my subjective criteria, let's take a short cut and define the terms *leader*, *great leader*, and *leadership* so we can identify leaders worth looking into (in my view).

Let's start with the term 'leader' from the oxfordlearnersdictionaries. com:

*'The person who leads or commands a group, organization, or country.'*

Well, that's not entirely helpful as it includes everyone that I just disqualified and considers people holding top tier positions without competence or without having earned the right to do so. We see that in both business and politics.

An easy example of the latter is where an heir takes over a country, usually from an already incompetent dictator. Kim Jong Un is just one of way too many examples, and this type of nepotism tends to make things worse. On the business end, there are (unfortunately) too many examples where incompetent 'leaders' have been given the top job, not based on merit, but who they are or know. I'm sure you have personally witnessed this on many occasions.

The bigger problem is that most people don't recognize their incompetency or that they didn't deserve the promotion or role. Give a person a business card stating CEO, and you will see that most cannot handle it; they will start to act *unnaturally* and try to live up to perceptions and expectations surrounding this title. This is further fueled by the people that surround them; a *posse* or *entourage* who laugh at jokes that aren't funny, agree regardless of their own opinions, and display a great deal of respect that has *not* been earned. All of this is, of course, on borrowed time. These temporary executives typically decline faster than products without preservatives, and they end up understanding that it was the CEO title that people 'honored', not them. This is what happens when you bestow that title of leadership on someone who hasn't the first clue. Moving on – we can eliminate all those people holding leadership positions without having earned them.

What about 'great leader'? Ah, much better! Now we start getting interesting definitions and criteria.

'A great leader means defining and exhibiting moral and ethical courage, and setting an example for everyone.' [1]

'A great leader is someone who communicates clearly, concisely, and often, and by doing so motivates everyone to give his or her best all the time. They challenge their people by setting high but attainable standards and expectations, and then giving them the support, tools, training, and latitude to pursue those goals and become the best employees they can possibly be.' [2]

'A great leader helps a group of people identify what they want and how to get it, and then influences that group, free of coercion, to take coordinated action to achieve the desired outcomes. A great leader achieves results at a level far beyond what others achieve.' [3]

I'm not entirely sure if these are the best definitions but they do provide a clearer picture.

Peter Drucker illustrates the difference between leaders and managers quite clearly:

'Management is doing things right; leadership is doing the right things.'

As you might recollect from Part I, the above was an overriding mantra in my consulting business as it has far reaching consequences. So many companies strive to do things right without having great leadership steering the course of the journey, and too late do they realize they simply did not do the right things – large conglomerates and the digital revolution is a great example of this. We had young leaders starting businesses that undermined large conglomerates unfortunately helmed by managers. Media companies followed by telecom and retail businesses lacked true leaders and are now suffering the consequences. Following my line of work over the years, financial companies seem to be following suit.

One of my favorite definitions of a great leader stems from my consulting days. I used the quote below in workshops held for CEOs, where my ultimate goal was simply to inspire them to become (better) leaders. Antoine de Saint-Exupery described a great leader as follows:

*'If you want to build a ship, don't drum up people to collect wood and don't assign them tasks and work, but rather teach them to long for the endless immensity of the sea.'*

In my mind, this is a great quote representing the focus of a great leader! In essence, a great leader inspires rather than dictates.

Now we come to leadership? What is leadership exactly? I found myself agreeing with the following:

*'A simple definition is that leadership is the art of motivating a group of people to act towards achieving a common goal.'* [4]

This leadership definition captures the essential concept – a leader inspires and leads others to achieve a broader vision. Effective leadership is based upon ideas (whether original or borrowed), but cannot take place unless those ideas are communicated to others in a way that engages them enough to act. In a nutshell, the leader is both inspiration and director of an action. He or she is the person that possesses that X factor, a combination of personality and leadership skills that almost compels others to follow their direction. Now that is a definition I can subscribe to. Armed with this, let's go back and see who best fits the label of 'greatest leaders'.

I chose the following two people as best examples of greatest business leaders:

**Bill Gates**

**Ingvar Kamprad**

And my picks for examples of greatest world leaders are:

**Nelson Mandela**

**Winston Churchill**

The reason why I picked the above will hopefully be clear as you read about them in the following pages. I would like to make one observation before I start: I chose four men. There have been many great female leaders throughout history, and this book is dedicated to my daughter so naturally I wanted to include a female figure. However, having read through many biographies, I realized that just about all of the leaders who had the largest impact, good or bad, have been men. Think about a female head of business that actively shaped and defined an industry or a female politician that had the same impact as that of Mandela or Churchill. Margaret Thatcher and Indira Gandhi are, no doubt, impressive. Rosa Parks and Mother Teresa were incredible activists. Cleopatra and Elizabeth I were commended for their leadership. So why didn't I include any women in this section? While exceptional female leaders exist(ed), they were not necessarily as many and not given the same opportunity as men, maybe easiest explained by the fact they have had a tougher time gaining a voice. This raises the question surrounding leadership skills: are these ingrained, perhaps developed through genetics or environment? Having read multiple research studies on this subject, I am convinced there are no inherited genetic differences relevant to leadership. On an interesting note, I truly believe the biggest obstacle in becoming a great leader is a person's ego. I am 100% convinced that every human being's greatest enemy is their ego, and though I haven't done any research to confirm or deny this, it always appeared (to me anyway) that men have much larger egos than women. Those of you who work in large corporate environments know what I mean – the politics and bullshit created by the 'mine is bigger than yours' culture. Women have a huge advantage here as, it appears, they aren't 'slaves' to their egos like men. In addition, traditional societal roles also give women a certain advantage where they might be more caring and reflective, among other things, than their male counterparts. Some of my female friends have hinted that male egos have prevented the rise of women parallel to men. What a shame; we could have had twice as many great leaders and made twice the progress in our world history, had men not blocked women.

As we need great leadership now more than ever, it's not an option to foster leaders in only half of the population. We all bear a shared responsibility to ensure female leaders emerge as we can all only benefit from this. My later conclusions might be derived from men (mainly) and a male perspective, but they apply equally to women.

# 14.
# BILL GATES

It's no surprise that Bill Gates pops up in 'top leaders', 'great leaders' or 'world leader' searches. There have been numerous books written about him and there is hardly a person alive today who is unfamiliar with his name. We know he co-founded Microsoft and turned the computer industry on its ear with MS-DOS and Windows. Through this, he became one of the richest people ever. It should be mentioned that, from the four leaders I have chosen, Bill Gates is the one where there is also loud criticism. His aggressive leadership style, tax optimization, and who his foundation has awarded is among just some of his criticism. But as you read through the following, I hope it will be clear why I have chosen him.

Bill Gates was born in Seattle in 1955 (he's a Scorpio for those who believe in astrology and traditional personality traits). His parents were well educated with his father a prominent lawyer while his mother served on the board of directors of First Interstate BancSystem and the United Way. She would often bring a young Bill to her volunteer work among schools and community organizations. He had a privileged upper-middle class upbringing with encouragement to seek higher education and develop a competitive spirit that aimed for excellence. During his early schooling years, he developed a strong interest in computing, and as luck would have it, his future partner and co-founder of Microsoft, Paul Allen, was his class mate. Bill was a voracious reader and excelled in nearly all his subjects, taking particular interest in math and science. At the age of 13, Bill drafted his first software program (we are talking 1968 here!) on the school's computer, and shortly afterwards, a tic-tac-toe program allowing users to play against the computer. As most 13-year-olds did not really come up with inventions beyond their years, this set him apart. A few years later, he and a few friends computerized a firm's payroll system and created a scheduling program for the school.

Bill and Paul grew quite close and spent most of their time programming together. Paul was (apparently) reserved and shy while Bill was feisty and somewhat combative. In 1970, at the tender ages of 15 and 17, Bill and Paul started a business together, Traf-o-Data, a computer program that monitored traffic patterns in Seattle, thus making their first $20,000.

Bills parents wanted him to study law, and in 1973 he went to Harvard (allegedly with a SAT score of 1590 out of 1600) while Paul went to Washington State University. After two years, Paul dropped out, around the same time Bill read an edition of *Popular Electronics* magazine that set him off on a mission. The article featured an Altair mini-computer kit that made Bill and Allen dream of possibilities that could be created in the world of Personal Computing. Bill and Paul spent two months writing a program for the Altair computer at the Harvard computer lab, eventually convincing the CEO of Altair that their program could run the Altair computer. In 1975, they founded Microsoft with Bill as head of the company. The BASIC software they developed became very popular with computer hobbyists, however these hobbyists reproduced and distributed the software for free (during this period, personal computer enthusiasts were not in it for the money i.e. the good old days...). Bill had the vision that only by allowing software developers to make a profit off their production, would innovation and good software for the future of computing be secured.

Microsoft's big break arrived in 1980 when IBM was looking for software to operate their upcoming personal computer (PC). Bill maximized this opportunity through a clever, strategic move where they became the exclusive licensing agent, and later, full owner of a software company that developed a program similar to what IBM required, although developed for other computers. IBM wanted to buy the source code Microsoft developed for the IBM PC, but Bill refused and thereby allowed Microsoft to license their MS-DOS to IBM, and later to any other potential upcoming PC manufacturers that would clone the IBM PC. Microsoft later developed software that could operate the Apple II machines, as Steve Jobs was focused on the hardware. The cooperation and knowledge-sharing between Apple and Microsoft, and the legendary rivalry between the pair, led Bill to develop Windows, a system using a mouse which beat Apple in the consumer market game. To pre-empt Apple, Bill made a huge splash announcing Microsoft was about to develop a graphic interface, compatible with all MS-DOS systems. Supposedly, Microsoft had no such program at the time but Bill made a bet that people running MS-DOS (comprising 30% of the market then) would wait for the new Microsoft Windows program. And he was right.

Two years later, in 1985, Windows launched to much success – this was two years after the launch of the Apple Macintosh, and in 1998, Microsoft launched Microsoft Office, which was another major breakthrough selling more than 100,000 copies in two weeks. Microsoft secured a virtual monopoly on operating systems for PCs and the rest is history.

Bill, with his intelligence, was able to foresee and understand all sides of the software industry. He was known to analyze possible strategic moves, all potential scenarios, and ask questions about anything that could happen. Apparently, despite his success, Bill never felt totally secure which kept him driven (or obsessed). This translated into a confrontational management style where employees would be challenged with feedback like, 'this is the most stupid idea I have ever heard'. This however was done out of passion, to get the best out of the employees, and see how passionate they themselves were.

He worked hard, even sleeping under his desk or re-writing code he was not satisfied with. In 2000, at the age of 45, Bill handed over his position of CEO to Steve Ballmer, in order to focus on Microsoft software architecture and the Bill and Melinda Gates Foundation (BMGF). In 2008, he retired from Microsoft and in 2014 he stepped down as the Chairman of Microsoft to focus on the foundation.

Bill Gates proved himself to be a great business man, strategist, and business leader with Microsoft, and also one of the few that step down voluntarily before getting (too) old. He was not done putting his leadership skills to work, and with the BMGF foundation he would prove to the world that he was not only a business leader but a world leader ready to tackle world problems. The William H. Gates Foundation was established in 1994 to tackle contemporary issues like education, world health, and to support low-income communities.

His wife, Melinda, and mother, Mary, can take credit for inspiring Bill to take a strong interest in charity. The knowledge that with great wealth comes great responsibility followed when he looked at individuals like Andrew Carnegie and John D. Rockefeller who, after becoming among the wealthiest people in the world, turned philanthropists.

In 2000, Bill and Melinda combined several family foundations, contributing $28 billion to the Bill and Melinda Gates Foundation that was focused on specific challenges, particularly within education and health. The foundation is run like a business with 'Goalkeepers' reporting on what goals have been met in areas such as child mortality, malnutrition, and HIV.

In 2017, Bill identified infections and chronic diseases as the two biggest public health concerns that needed to be addressed over the next decade. In 2018, Bill teamed up with Larry Page (co-founder of Google) to fund a universal flu vaccine. Bill has further dedicated resources to developing a cure for Alzheimer's as well as the development of a 'smart city' (Belmont) dedicated to the creation of a forward-thinking community.

These projects are visionary with a huge impact hereto unseen on this scale, projects that a world leader would only dream of taking on and funding at his own cost. I have first-hand experience with charity as my wife started our foundation, Future4Children in 2005. It is difficult, frustrating, emotional, and takes uncompromising commitment to see it through. To be fair, my wife took that on but I was allowed to experience the pleasure, the tremendous pleasure, one experiences when you actually change things for the better. In our case, it was education for the underprivileged children in developing countries. My wife has always stated, 'Money can actually buy happiness – by giving it away.' Maybe this is Bills' true calling...

In 2010, Bill took another huge step up in terms of using his leadership skills. The Giving Pledge, defined by Bill as 'an effort to help address society's most pressing problems by inviting the world's wealthiest individuals and families to commit more than half of their wealth to philanthropy or charitable causes either during their lifetime or in their will'. Now this is HUGE. Think about it – giving away over half your wealth that has likely been accumulated over generations or through incredibly hard work. Just giving it away...

The idea is something many of us have thought about. The execution is a different story, and grandiose in nature exhibiting world class leadership that goes way beyond developing excellent software.

I need to explain it in more detail (quoting their website www. givingpledge.org/): *'In August 2010, 40 of America's wealthiest individuals and couples joined together in a commitment to give more than half of their wealth away. Created by Bill and Melinda Gates and Warren Buffett, the Giving Pledge came to life following a series of conversations with philanthropists around the world about how they could collectively set a new standard of generosity among the ultra-*

*wealthy. The Giving Pledge is a simple concept: an open invitation for billionaires, or those who would be if not for their giving, to publicly dedicate the majority of their wealth to philanthropy. And it is inspired by the example set by millions of people at all income levels who give generously, often at great personal sacrifice, to make the world better. Envisioned as a multi-generational effort, the Giving Pledge aims over time to help shift the social norms of philanthropy toward giving more, giving sooner, and giving smarter. Those who join the Giving Pledge often write a letter explaining their decision to engage deeply and publicly in philanthropy, as well as describing the philanthropic causes to which they are devoted. Signatories give to a diverse range of issues including poverty alleviation, refugee aid, disaster relief, global health, education, women and girls' empowerment, medical research, arts and culture, criminal justice reform, and environmental sustainability. While originally focused on the United States, the Giving Pledge quickly saw interest from philanthropists around the world. Today, the pledge includes 183 of the world's wealthiest individuals, couples, and families, ranging in age from their 30s to their 90s. Globally, they represent 22 countries: Australia, Brazil, Canada, China (mainland and Taiwan), Cyprus, Germany, India, Indonesia, Israel, Malaysia, Monaco, Norway, Russia, Saudi Arabia, Slovenia, South Africa, Tanzania, Turkey, Ukraine, UAE, the United Kingdom, and the United States. The Giving Pledge also provides a forum for some of the world's most engaged philanthropists to discuss challenges, successes and failures, and how to be smarter about giving. People who have joined the pledge are united by a shared commitment to learning and giving, and they have opportunities to gather throughout the year to learn from experts about how best to leverage their philanthropy to address some of the world's biggest challenges'.*

This is a major, take-your-hat-off accomplishment that will change the world, and it was Bill who did it. His first stop was Warren Buffet who, apparently, said yes. This must have cemented his belief that it was doable. Through his dedication and leadership, it came true.

My wife always stated at the Future4Children fundraising events, that world poverty is solvable and will have to be solved. She would state (before imagining how quickly she would be proven right) that if not solved, there would be no ocean deep enough and no wall high enough, to keep the poorest from migrating to countries where wealth is concentrated. She would further argue that our generation had simply chosen not to solve the poverty issue, and if we all donated what we spent on ice cream alone, some of the greatest poverty issues could be solved. Well, Bill went and took that step, and I think history will recognize him more for these results than for building Microsoft. He turned from business leader to world leader, and with his positive contribution to mankind goes down in my book as a *great* leader.

# 15.
# INGVAR KAMPRAD

I chose Ingvar Kamprad based on his unique leadership style and personality. Known as the Founder of IKEA, which made him one of the wealthiest men in the world, he is a tad more difficult to describe than the other leaders I've selected here. Multiple attributes make him one of the greatest business leaders ever so let's get to know the man behind the scenes.

Ingvar (as he liked to be called) was born in Sweden in 1926 to a Swedish mother and a German father. Though he grew up on a farm, he showed early signs of exceptional business acumen. He started selling matches at the age of five, and by seven realized that if he bicycled to neighboring towns (thereby selling more), he could buy the matches in bulk and save on the extra costs. We later see that this was one of the key ideas that defined IKEA's success.

Over the next few years, he expanded his supply range e.g. he took out a loan of SEK 500 (around $50 US) to bulk purchase pens from Paris and sold them in Sweden at a good profit. This was the last time he took out a loan. At the tender age of 17, his father gave him a gift of cash as a reward for his studies. It was at this time that he founded IKEA instead of continuing with his education. This might have come as a surprise to his father but his teachers understood as they had struggled to teach Ingvar simple basics like reading. Little did they know he was Dyslexic.

Initially, IKEA sold replicas of kitchen tables through mail order, expanding into other products. It was in this period that he made what he would later call, 'the most stupid mistake of my life' as he helped raise funds for a fascist group in Sweden. Never the less, his key focus was building up and expanding IKEA, driven by his mission to provide beautiful but very affordable furniture to the average home. At the time, furniture was a luxury item many people couldn't afford. He opened a store and to attract prospective customers, he promised a free cup of coffee and bun to anyone who showed up. To his own surprise, more than a thousand people attended and that was the seed that sprouted combining food and restaurants as an integral part of IKEA stores. I vividly remember my excitement as a kid when making a trip to the IKEA store in order to buy things for my room, *and* to eat a meal there.

Ingvar was obsessed with finding the most 'cost effective' way to produce furniture with the idea that 'it's better to sell 500 chairs at a lower price than 50 chairs at a high price'. His business practice did not go unnoticed with his competitors, of which many also were suppliers, and most of them decided to boycott IKEA. The Swedish Federation of Wood and Furniture was so outraged by his 'price dumping' that they persuaded logging firms to stop supplying IKEA. But Ingvar was on a mission so rather than let them kill his business, he figured out a way to get supplies from their cheaper neighbor, Poland, instead – a rather unusual idea at that time. In 1960, he travelled to the US and saw how the Cash & Carry system worked and, shortly after returning to Sweden, opened a 31,000 sqm IKEA store, much like we know them today, where customers choose, pay, and carry their flat pack furniture away, drive home, and assemble it. He was convinced Sweden was at the forefront of a car boom and therefore decided to open his stores in suburban areas to keep costs low and offer decent parking spaces. In addition, to encourage people to save money by transporting their own furniture, he started offering roof racks at outrageously low prices. He took the Cash & Carry system but significantly improved it – that became a key pillar of his success. His furniture was also given names as he had difficulties with numbers, a concept that remains today.

With a proven concept, Ingvar set his sights on the overseas markets and opened stores in the Scandinavian region in 1963, continuing a rapid global expansion to 313 stores in 38 countries today. This makes IKEA the world's leading furniture company with 533 million people visiting its stores on a yearly basis and a sales volume estimated at over $24 billion. Its catalogue once had a print run of 150 million copies and it has been claimed that roughly 10% of the European population have been conceived in an IKEA bed.

You have to wonder about his focus and determination. His rise to success is not like Bill Gates who developed much needed software that was embedded in all computers. We are talking about furniture, chairs, and tables that most people could build or produce themselves. Obviously, it takes dedication and Ingvar had that in spades, which is reflected in his quote, 'If you work and do not feel enthusiasm, consider that at least a third of your life has gone down the drain'. But he was also obsessed; obsessed with quality and cost. As a good leader, he walked the talk. He drove an old Volvo, flew economy class, and encouraged IKEA employees to use both sides of the page. Supposedly, he would use a tea bag twice and often had meals at IKEA. He purchased Christmas gifts on sale *after* Christmas. A friend of mine who was engaging with IKEA stayed in super cheap hotels, as did the management of IKEA themselves. Ingvar stated, 'it is not only for cost reasons that we avoid the luxury hotels. We do not need flashy cars, impressive titles, uniforms, or other status symbols. We rely on our strength and will'.

The man was obsessed with costs. Think about that for a moment: If IKEA sell over 100 million pieces of furniture every year each with say 20 screws, and you find a way to cut the length of the screws by about one third, that's a substantial saving! With a volume business based on low price, everything mattered and management were constantly trying to save costs. Ingvar actually published a few notable works around this notion, such as *A Testament of a Furniture Dealer'* in 1976.

He was a highly detailed person and added his personal touch wherever possible. He spent most of his time visiting stores, walking around in search of things to improve. He was a very charismatic leader and stated, 'If there is such a thing as good leadership, it is to give a good example' and 'I have to do so for all IKEA employees'. He treated staff all over the world as family and always hugged all employees, whomever and wherever. He met with employees from all levels of the hierarchy and managed to create an authentic family atmosphere in a company with around 200,000 employees. His values consisted of humility, the confidence to admit weakness, quality, heritage, market differences, customer loyalty, and sustainability – all of which are deeply embedded in the global IKEA culture and influenced decision making in every department on a daily basis. That is leadership at a great level. His long-term vision of furnishing entire homes, by delivering on what really matters to the customers, is a uniquely IKEA idea and likely to carry the company forward after his death on January 27th 2018. He set up the company through a foundation to ensure its independence for generations to come. Ingvar followed Bill Gates' pledge and stated in his will that half of his estate should go to charity, namely to projects in a sparsely populated area of Sweden.

His story sounds amazing but we must remember that Ingvar was not perfect - nobody is. He would often state that 'no one has had as many fiascos as I have' and went through many boycotts, struggles with his past involvement with Nazism, tax avoidance, plagiarism, and alcoholism. He thought it alien if things went too smoothly and it almost seemed fitting that his personal character was born to struggle and fight against a complacent life.

Ingvar built the world's leading furniture company and became one of the wealthiest people to date, however it is his humility, his passion, his way to inspire employees that makes him one of the greatest business leaders of all times.

# 16.
# NELSON MANDELA

It's no surprise that Nelson Mandela pops up in every 'top world leader' search, usually among the top 15. A few years ago, my daughter had to make a presentation about him to her 9th grade class. I would have loved to simply insert what she had produced, unfortunately it was a presentation and she said, 'Daddy, you have to do your own work!'

Most people know the basic story of Mandela's anti-apartheid activism leading to his long imprisonment, and later his ascension as the first black President of South Africa. Let's not forget his Nobel peace prize! But to understand him as a leader, we need to recount the highlights of his life, especially his political life. This is no easy task as no one in our history has so restlessly spent their entire life on achieving one mission. Fasten your seat belt as we speed through an amazing life story.

Mandela was born in 1918 in the South African village, Mvezo. He was given the name Rolihlahla, meaning troublemaker in the local language. Little did his mother know how aptly that name suited him. His great grandfather had been the King of the Thembu people; however, as Mandela's mother was from the Ixhiba clan, Mandela's family branch was ineligible to inherit the throne (though recognized as hereditary royal councilors). Mandela's father was a local chief and councilor to the monarch. Both parents were illiterate and none of the children had attended school. Mandela was the first to do so and in school the teacher gave him an English name, Nelson (which to my knowledge simply means son of Neil so likely just an arbitrary name). After his father's early death, Mandela's mother went to the Thembu regent and entrusted him with guardianship over Mandela, which meant he spent his teenage years in the 'Great Place' palace. This, one can assume, must have been somewhat inspiring. At the age of 17, Mandela moved to a college in Fort Beaufort where he deepened his interest in African history and culture, and became friends with a Sotho native and a teacher who had no trouble breaking taboos.

At the age of 21, he started his BA degree at the University of Fort Hare, an elite black institution where he, among other subjects, studied politics and Dutch law. It was here that he met, someone who would become his lifelong friend, Oliver Tambo. He became very involved with the Student Representative Council but was suspended from school after initiating a boycott (making his original name meaningful). He never returned. Around the same time, a marriage had been arranged on his behalf but he was clever enough to flee to Johannesburg. There, he stayed with a cousin who introduced him to an ANC activist who helped him get a job in a law firm. He became friends with several ANC sympathizers and attended communist gatherings. He was (supposedly) very impressed that Europeans, Africans, and Indians mixed as equals there but did not join the party as he did not see the South African struggle as a class warfare, but rather one based on racial bias. In 1943, he finally completed his BA exams (giving up was not in his nature) and later went to study law at University of Witwatersrand, where he was the only black student and faced racism on a daily basis. Not surprising in the least, he became politically involved and joined the ANC, along with Oliver Tambo. He soon illustrated exceptional leadership skills as he helped found the ANC Youth League (ANCYL) in 1944 and took a seat on the executive committee. With that, his political career had started and he discontinued his law studies.

In 1950, Mandela was elected president of the ANCYL and also became an executive member at the ANC. With increasing apartheid and segregation laws, Mandela reflected on the situation and eventually took the stance that a multi-racial front would be more effective. He was also drawn to the idea of a classless society, a Marxist philosophy, but wanted to follow a similar path carved by Mahatma Gandhi (another great leader) where non-violent resistance along with boycotts and strikes were used. In 1952, Mandela spoke at a rally consisting of 10,000 people but was immediately arrested and briefly interned. This episode established him as one of the important black political leaders of the time. A few months later, he was arrested again and sentenced to nine months hard labor on the grounds of 'statutory communism', a term used for opposing the apartheid movement. In 1953 his speech 'No easy walk to freedom' was read at an ANC meeting. The speech laid out a plan (referred to as the M-plan) for how the ANC could continue their struggle in an environment where they would be banned. Mandela also established the only native South African-run law firm with Tambo, as Mandela had passed his attorney qualification exams. Most of the cases they worked on revolved around police brutality and they were constantly harassed by the authorities.

In 1955, after realizing their political struggle was inefficient, Mandela started to believe that violent action was the only means to ending apartheid. The following years were consumed with the state's law suits against the ANC and Mandela, but they successfully defended themselves against most of the charges. This led to the prosecutor filing for high treason. In 1959, responding to the unrest, the state implemented a state of emergency, declaring martial law and banning the ANC – something Mandela had foreseen many years before. Mandela was thrown in prison for five months without trial. In 1961, the government suffered an embarrassing defeat as the high treason charge ended with a 'not guilty' verdict. Mandela started travelling around the country, organizing the new ANC cell structure as laid out in his M-plan. At the same time, a new order was issued for his arrest. Mandela felt that it was time for a stronger struggle and formed the 'Spear of the Nation' militant group, known as the Umkhonto we Sizwe or MK, to engage in guerrilla warfare. The MK started to carry out acts of sabotage that would exert maximum pressure on the government with minimum casualties. These included attacking power plants, military installations, telephone lines and other critical infrastructure where and/or when civilians were not present. In 1962, Mandela went on a trip to a dozen countries in order to rally support for the ANC's case with politicians, journalists and, of course, other activists. Upon his return to South Africa, he was captured by the police, supposedly on a tip received from the CIA. His court case was widely followed and Mandela, instead of calling witnesses, used the opportunity to clearly state his political cause. He was sentenced to five years.

While Mandela was in prison, police raided several ANC homes and eventually charged Mandela (again) and several others with treason. Several trials followed, one of which featured Mandela's legendary three-hour speech, 'I am prepared to die' which raised support for him around the globe. In 1964, he was sentenced to life in prison, to be served at Robben Island. His cell was damp and measured five square meters. Mandela was treated harshly by both white inmates and the prison guards, spending much time in solitary confinement, and was only allowed one letter and visit every six months. Over the years, conditions improved and Mandela started communicating more with the outside world, sending his life story (among other documents) to London. Political support increased around the world. He was given awards in multiple countries and in 1980, the slogan 'Free Mandela' was developed, sparking an international campaign. It also sparked increased violence in South Africa, combined with a stagnate economy due to many countries instituting sanctions against South Africa. Eventually, in 1985, the government feeling immense pressure, offered Mandela his release if he would denounce violence as a political weapon. Mandela rejected the offer, stating 'What freedom am I being offered while the organization of the people (ANC) remains banned? Only free men can negotiate.' This led to increased violence and sabotage placing further pressure on the apartheid government. A new offer was made to Mandela in 1988. Again, Mandela declined, saying the ANC would only end their armed struggle once the government renounced violence. Think about that for a moment. Mandela rejected freedom after 24 years in prison! Now that is a leader putting his people before himself.

In 1989, de Klerk took over the presidency of South Africa and under him, things changed fast as he believed apartheid was unsustainable. He invited Mandela to a meeting and shortly after legalized all former banned parties, as well as announcing Mandela's unconditional release in February 1990. Mandela's release from prison was broadcasted live across the world. He made a speech in which he committed to a reconciliation with the white minority but also stated that armed struggle would continue as a purely defensive action against the violence of apartheid until the black majority were given the right to vote. Soon after, he went on a long trip to meet the heads of leading countries, rallying support for his cause. Upon his return, Mandela offered the government a ceasefire to negotiate majority rule and he was elected president of the ANC.

In 1993, negotiations took a positive turn with an interim constitution based on liberal democracy, and de Klerk and Mandela were awarded the Nobel peace prize. The ANC started campaigning with Mandela as their key speaker, and in 1994, after a campaign littered with struggle and violent reactions, the ANC won a clear majority in the country's first democratic elections where Mandela became the President of South Africa. No leader has personally suffered and been terrorized as much as Mandela (although Trump claims he has...).

In the end, he won, but let's ponder this for a moment. South Africa had been ruled by a privileged, white minority, and now a party without experience has to create a functioning government but also live up to high expectations. This is not a job anyone would normally desire but Mandela took this in his stride and went on to prove himself as a leader of state.

In transforming from apartheid to a multicultural democracy, Mandela's first priority was that of national reconciliation. De Klerk was given the position of Deputy President and Mandela allowed him to stay in the presidential residence while he stayed in a manor he renamed 'Genadendal', meaning 'Valley of Mercy.' Mandela lived simply, donating a third of his income to the Nelson Mandela Children's Fund which he founded in 1995. He also (finally) published his autobiography, Long Walk to Freedom.

Mandela was fully aware of the impact faced by other post-colonial African economies that were damaged by the departure of white elites, and therefore worked to reassure the white population that they were protected and represented within the 'rainbow nation.' He went on to appoint several former National Party officials as ministers. Mandela encouraged black South Africans to forgive for the sake of peace and to get behind the previously hated national rugby team during the Rugby World Cup taking place in Ellis Park, South Africa in 1995. Mandela sported the team's official shirt and after the team won the championship, he presented the trophy to the (mostly) white team. With this, Mandela won the hearts of millions of the white rugby fans, to the dismay of the black militants. He oversaw the formation of the Truth and Reconciliation Commission to investigate crimes under apartheid and to avoid the creation of martyrs. He ensured individual amnesties in exchange for testimony of the crimes committed. For Mandela, this was the key to move beyond the past and focus on the present and future.

Mandela's administration inherited a country with a huge wealth disparity between blacks and whites, where much of the native African population lived under the poverty line. Mandela decided to place emphasis on economic growth through market economics and encouragement of foreign investments. This went against the common desire of the ANC who wanted to address social inequality immediately. Still, under Mandela, blacks got free health care, children were brought into the educational system, millions were connected to electricity and three million got access to housing and water.

However, another problem was brewing: the exodus of thousands of skilled whites who wanted to escape the increased crime and higher taxes. Mandela publicly criticized those who simply left and exerted leadership abilities beyond solving issues within South Africa alone. He tried to assist other nations in solving conflicts through diplomacy and reconciliation, and calling for an African renaissance. Although Mandela governed decisively, he started delegating duties and responsibilities and, shortly before his 80th birthday, stepped down as president of the ANC. Although the constitution allowed him to run for another four years, he announced his resignation as president in 1999, shortly before the next election. At that point, he enjoyed an 80% approval rating among all voters.

His retirement was widely regarded as a semi-retirement as he reverted to a busy public life, meeting with world leaders and being very active with his foundation. In 2004, with failing health, he finally 'retired from retirement' and retreated from public life. Never the less, he convened a group of world leaders to use their knowledge and experiences to address some of the world's toughest problems. On his 90th birthday, he held a speech in which he called for the rich to help the poor, 'It is time for new hands to lift the burdens. It is in your hands now.'2 He successfully campaigned for South Africa to host the 2010 FIFA World Cup, declaring it would be a gift for his nation. After suffering from a prolonged lung infection, Mandela died in 2013. Approximately 90 foreign state dignitaries attended his funeral in South Africa, honoring him as one of the world's greatest leaders.

As I mentioned in the beginning, many books have been written about him, highlighting his pragmatic political approach rather than that of an intellectual scholar or political theorist. His charismatic leadership style magnetized people because he always looked for the best in others. He once stated, 'I was not a messiah but an ordinary man who had become a leader because of extraordinary circumstances.' Well, it's classic that a great man like Mandela would downplay himself while narcissistic leaders are busy shouting out on their 'great and unmatched wisdom'.3

# 17.
# WINSTON CHURCHILL

Winston Churchill was the Prime Minister of Great Britain during the Second World War and is credited with playing a vital role in making sure most of the world do not now speak German as a first language or have sausages as their national delight. In a 2002 BBC survey, he was voted number one in the Greatest Britons of all times. His life was long, complex, and controversial with a great deal of drama. His colorful, controversial statements like, 'religion is a delicious narcotic' put him at odds with many people and institutions. To really appreciate his brilliance, particularly his foresight and strategic ability, we will need to go into a detailed description. As you read on, I believe it will become clear that he was an outstanding leader – no matter how you define it.

Churchill was born in 1874 into an aristocratic family at a time when the United Kingdom was the dominant world power. His father had been a Member of Parliament and his mother hailed from an extremely wealthy American family. Aged seven, he went to boarding school but reportedly often misbehaved. Narrowly passing the entrance exam for the elite Harrow School, he began studying there in 1888. He excelled in academics, especially history, but his teachers complained he was unpunctual and careless, and he performed poorly in his exams. On his father's insistence, he pursued a military education and, after three attempts, succeeded in being admitted to the Royal Military Academy at Sandhurst in 1893. Churchill was eager to witness military action and in 1895 travelled to Cuba and joined the Spanish troops. A year later he was posted to India, 'a godless land of snobs and bores', according to him. At that time, he began a project of self-education, reading Plato, Adam Smith, Darwin and Henry Hallam. He took a keen interest in British parliamentary affairs and declared himself a Liberal in all but name.

In 1899, at the age of 24, Churchill decided he wanted a political career. He started giving addresses at Conservative Party meetings and was selected as a parliamentary candidate that same year, but lost. He then went to South Africa for the Boer War, where he was appointed Lieutenant in the South African Horse Regiment. After victory in Pretoria, he went back to Britain where he revived his political campaigning and won a seat in Parliament (Conservatives) at the age of 25. As politicians were not paid at that time, he travelled around and made speeches, for which he was paid. Through his travel activity, he met President McKinley of the US and dined with Vice President, Theodore Roosevelt.

In 1891, he had started making his mark on politics with his maiden speech in the House of Commons but soon started socializing with the Liberals and voted with them on social issues. He also started to entertain the idea of forming a central party uniting Conservatives and Liberals. His increasing criticism of the Conservatives and their leader angered many Conservatives and it was 'decided' no support would flow to his campaign in the next election and he defected to the Liberal party. Churchill stood up for his beliefs, not for the party, and this made him a unique politician and true political leader. In 1906, the Liberals won the election and Churchill became Under Secretary of State for the Colonial Office at the age of 32. Recall that the Colonies during that time period were a big thing for the empire where the sun never sets. The position enabled him to travel and see the world for himself.

In 1908, aged 34, Churchill was promoted to the Cabinet as President of the Board of Trade. Though he was the youngest

Cabinet member, he championed social reform and his speeches were published in the volumes *Liberalism and the Social Problem* and *The Peoples Rights*. The House of Lords tried to block these initiatives but Churchill stood by his beliefs, arguing that these upper-class obstructions could fuel a class war. He therefore proposed the abolition of the House of Lords. It should be noted that membership in the House of Lords was an entitlement of all hereditary peers, the ultimate elitist system. Under the House of Lords Act in 1999, the right to membership was restricted to 92 hereditary peers 'only'. Since 2008, only one of those members is female as most hereditary peerages can only be inherited by men. The United Kingdom, as it stands, are way behind in so many ways – we can only applaud Churchill for being a century ahead of his peers when he brought this proposal!

In 1910, Churchill was promoted to Home Secretary, where he immediately introduced more social reforms. This included throwing his support behind voting rights for women (only if the male majority agreed, of course). Switzerland, my home country, waited until 1971 to give women voting rights at a national level.

In 1911, as the Agadir crisis emerged and threatened war between Germany and France, Churchill suggested that the UK should form an alliance with France and Russia to safeguard the independence of Belgium, the Netherlands, and Denmark. He wanted peaceful negotiations first but also began promoting a much stronger Royal Navy, foreseeing the importance this would play in a conflict. He was appointed First Lord of the Admiralty by the Prime Minister and spent the next two and a half years on naval preparations. As tension built, Germany passed a law increasing the production of warships. Churchill proclaimed that for every one they built; Britain would build two. He ordered the building of 100 'seaplanes' as he termed them and started taking flying lessons himself. He was pursuing a belief with passion, and it later turned out to be a decisive one. At the time though, he was considered a lone wolf pushing an agenda and had to convince everyone else. When one of his proposals to construct four new battleships was rejected, he threatened resignation as he did not believe there would be meaning in compromise. As a true strategist, he started planning security measures around fuel sources for the naval fleet, and in 1914 he convinced the House of Commons to purchase 51% of the Anglo-Persian Oil Company that ensured a secure oil supply for the Royal Navy.

As Germany invaded Belgium, Churchill took charge of naval warfare. He got 120,000 British troops across the channel to France, made a naval blockade of German North Sea ports and sent submarines to the Baltic Sea to support the Russians against the German war ships. Having proven his strategic shrewdness, he was also put in charge of aerial defense and became one of only four members of the War Council. In 1915, he made a surprising move and resigned from Government and the War Council, as he felt his energies and skills were not being fully utilized. As a capable leader, he wanted to do more, while remaining a Member of Parliament, he took up senior positions in the British Army to put his stamp on the front line. His involvement in 36 skirmishes put his life at risk, but Churchill was (supposedly) unconcerned.

After the War had ended, he returned to Britain and was appointed Secretary of State for War and Secretary of State of Air. Over the next five years, he worked as a politician and accepted the post of Chancellor of the Exchequer and formally re-joined the Conservative party with the words 'anyone can rat, but it takes a certain ingenuity to re-rat'. In his new post, he was to make what he later described as the biggest mistake of his life: a disastrous return to the gold standard and the pre-war exchange rate that threw Britain into financial tumult with depressed industries. In the 1929 election, the Conservative party lost and Churchill hit the 'wilderness years' of his political career. He spent the next few years writing, openly sharing his political views and opinions, ultimately becoming Britain's highest paid writer.

It was during this time frame that another great leader, Ghandi, crossed his path. Ghandi was on my short list of great leaders for this book due to his passive resistance movement and achievements, but Churchill saw him differently in those days. He saw Ghandi as a real threat to India's stability and the British economy, should independence be granted. He stated in a speech, 'It is alarming and also nauseating to see Mr. Ghandi, a seditious Middle Temple lawyer, now posing as a fakir of a type well known in the East, striding half naked up the steps of the Vice-regal palace to parley on equal terms with representatives of the King Emperor'. Wow, those are strong words indeed but that is exactly what made Ghandi a great leader. A lawyer from a modest background whose cause made him an equal in negotiations with the King of the superpower at the time. It raises many issues about how leaders view each other, especially when they cross paths.

In the summer of 1930, Churchill floated the visionary idea of a United States of Europe. The idea was termed 'outrageous' and didn't gain momentum. At the start of 1931, Churchill stood behind the idea of reconciliation between Germany and France, but was against Germany rearming herself – again, he stood as a lone wolf with this opinion. In 1934, he gave a major speech on defense, stressing the need for Britain to rebuild the Royal Air Force and to create a Ministry of Defence. Based on his views and where he saw the world was heading in the years to come, he kept his focus on these issues. A number of ministers stressed that Hitler's intentions were unclear, whereas Churchill wanted 25–30% of the British industry to be brought under state control for purposes of rearming themselves.

In 1936, Churchill ended up clashing with Baldwin in the House of Commons and he took the consequences and left, becoming extremely vocal in pushing for rearming against Germany and soon stating that Britain faced a choice between war or shame. Eventually, on September 3rd 1939, Britain declared war on Germany and Churchill was appointed First Lord of the Admiralty and member of the War Cabinet, the same positions he held during World War I. Churchill put forth a strategy that would obstruct German military operations, among others, by suggesting mining Norwegian waters to prevent iron ore from reaching Germany. Unfortunately, the remaining members of the War Cabinet and the French government initially disagreed on this strategy, and only approved it on April 8th 1940, which was too late as Germany invaded Norway 24 hours later. The failure with Norway forced Prime Minister Chamberlain's resignation and he advised the King to appoint someone who could command the support of all three major parties in the House of Commons during these times. Subsequently, King George VI offered the position to Churchill, which he accepted, stating that, at the age of 65, he was the only world leader from World War I holding a top political position in World War II. Like many great leaders when facing their biggest challenge, Churchill was focused and energized. His friends noticed the difference, saying he had become 20 years younger. His energy was contagious, filtering down to the entire population.

Throughout the War, Churchill suffered heart attacks, depression, and declining health, but he would soldier on aided by whiskey and cigars, ultimately travelling 160,000 km during the War. He was on a mission and nothing would stop him, not health and certainly not Hitler.

Churchill, with his clear views and rhetoric, had prepared Britain and her population for a long war. While he was not convinced of victory, and often joked that he would be dead in three months, he did everything possible to make sure that Britain would win. He appointed himself as the Minister of Defence, making him the much-needed match for Hitler's powers. In his first speech as Prime Minister, he stated, 'I have nothing to offer but blood, toil, tears, and sweat'. In another speech he stated, 'Let us brace ourselves to our duties and so bear ourselves, that if the British Empire and its Commonwealth last for a thousand years, men will say, "this was their finest hour."'

He inspired the population and Parliament with Britain fully committed and mobilized. Churchill did more than talk, and one of his first actions was to appoint a competent business man to gear up the production of war planes, which ultimately proved a key for victory. This was one out of many clever, strategic moves he undertook, and that strategic brilliance combined with stubbornness pushed Britain to punch above her limitations.

Churchill's relationship with US President Roosevelt proved very helpful and Roosevelt helped provide military hardware, oil, and munitions, as well as secure vital food supplies for Britain and her army. When Pearl Harbor was attacked, Churchill's first thought was that now they would win the War because the US would fight on their side.

As early as 1943, Churchill started to focus on world order post war, and started drafting his vision for a post-war world with treaties and borders. He was convinced that Germany would lose the War but also realized they needed to ensure a smooth transformation into stability. Churchill was highly respected by other world leaders, earning their support. He despised Stalin but in the interest of the War dealt with him in a very pragmatic way. When it came time to discuss post-war Europe with Stalin, Churchill simply suggested, 'Let us settle about our affairs in the Balkans. Your armies are in Rumania and Bulgaria. We have interests, missions, and agents there. Don't let us get at cross-purposes in small ways. So far as Britain and Russia are concerned, how would it do for you to have ninety per cent predominance in Rumania, for us to have ninety per cent of the say in Greece, and go fifty–fifty about Yugoslavia?'2 Churchill's clear, pragmatic, visionary initiatives made the Russians call him the 'British Bulldog'.

Churchill was a strong leader with a clear perception of what was necessary to win the War and followed through on his beliefs, even when meeting opposition at home. The biggest decision was that of the June 1944 Allied Invasion of Normandy. Movies have been made about this brutal battle from June 6th to August 30th and resulted in a total loss of 425,000 lives. For any leader to make such a decision is not easy and throughout history, we have seen political leaders avoiding hard decisions ending in long crises followed by tremendous suffering. In this case, Germany soon conceded defeat. On Victory Day, W spoke to a huge crowd and stated, 'This is your victory' to which the crowd shouted back, 'No, it is yours'.

During World War II, we saw great leadership working together to defeat a common enemy. Though Hitler and others had great leadership skills, they were anything but great leaders.

Without an election taking place for almost a decade, Churchill resigned as Prime Minister but in 1951 he was (again) appointed Prime Minster and his focus shifted to improving life for the masses with initiatives like housing and taxes until he resigned in 1955. He died 10 years later from a severe stroke.

Churchill was an amazing and visionary strategist, driven by passion with faith in his own judgement. If that meant shifting political parties, he would do so. For him, it was not about politics and parties, it was about doing the right thing; exactly what leaders are supposed to do! Although a controversial figure, his achievements are endless and he had a huge global following, many of whom remember him today.

# 18.
# WHAT DOES IT TAKE TO BE A GREAT LEADER?

Looking back at the four leaders I have described, certain characteristics stand out.

Firstly, they all had a clear passion, vision, or purpose. Nelson Mandela wanted to end apartheid and ensure equality for all South Africans. Bill Gates wants to make the world a better place, especially for the less privileged. Ingvar Kamprad wanted to give everyone a chance to own good quality, affordable furniture. Winston Churchill wanted to save the British Empire and the world from Hitler. Hitler had a purpose as well, albeit not a worthy one. Throughout history, leaders with a non-worthy purpose have in the end always lost their cause.

Secondly, our four leaders all possessed great communication skills. Churchill and Mandela are known for some of the most impactful speeches ever written. It's not clear if they were natural communicators, but if you're passionate about something, exercising your communication skills is a given if you're interested in achieving your purpose.

Thirdly, they all inspired people and have or had a great following. Bill Gates got 183 of the wealthiest people to join his Giving Pledge. Nelson Mandela got the majority of the nation as well as many world leaders and their nations to support his cause. Ingvar Kamprad got around 200,000 employees to follow and live his low-cost mantra. Churchill inspired nations to follow his lead to win the War. Now this is where the great leaders versus the rest are set apart. To gain a huge following without threats, without violence, without use of force means you inspire people to voluntarily support and fight for your cause. And for political leaders, that means you uniting rather than dividing people.

Fourth, our great leaders relentlessly follow their purpose, often at an obsessive level. This means they are not willing to compromise, and they are willing to personally suffer in achieving their purpose. Churchill's convictions put him at odds again and again with the establishment, but he would not compromise, even if that meant he would lose his position. Mandela was offered release from jail but was not willing to give in to the compromise and therefore stayed in jail without any hope of release. Bill Gates relentlessly followed his dream of building better operating systems which made him a demanding and sometimes difficult boss. And Ingvar Kamprad relentlessly drove down the cost of every little item in IKEA to achieve his purpose of making IKEA furniture affordable for all. All four men worked extremely hard and set their purpose above themselves. All, barring Mandela, could have easily settled for a nice life at a relatively early stage but they didn't: they were leaders with a purpose. By contrast, managers and CEOs are often happy to 'give up' one company and switch to another if the challenge is too tough (or the firm offers a higher pay check). That might be justifiable if you change industry but not if you change to a competitor. Throughout my career, I have never hired a potential employee that had worked at two competitors. These people had no credibility with me as I would see them for what they are: just interested in chasing titles and money. They have no purpose and they give up, exactly the opposite of a real leader. Some of the best CEOs I have met have been in their position for a very long time, and that often goes hand-in-hand with them having a purpose or passion. The majority of CEOs come in and hold a position for an average of three to four years, in which time they simply manage the firm, displaying no leadership skills whatsoever.

In addition to the above key characteristics, our chosen four also took risks, often breaking with the trend. If they spotted opportunities, they took them. They were charismatic, walked the talk, and were authentic.

*Being authentic* is a leadership characteristic, not a leadership skill. It's realizing who you are and daring to be who you are and doing what you believe you should be doing. The reason why I like to highlight this leadership trait is because this is where most managers or assholes totally fail. And there is a reason for this which I alluded to earlier: their ego.

Our ego is looking for identification and makes us believe *having* is *being*. In short, I have, therefore I am. I have a CEO title, I am important. I have these shoes, I am cool. I have this car; I am rich and respected. And then as a consequence, the more I have the more I am. The ego looks at this on a relative basis, relative to others that is, meaning the ego lives through comparison. As a consequence, how you are seen by others becomes how you see yourself. The ego's sense of self-worth is linked to the worth you have in the eyes of others, and you need others for your ego to get a sense of self. Because you compare yourself to others, your ego will seek to give you a higher self-esteem by looking down at others, complaining about others, talking bad about others and calling them names. Your ego seeks for you to be right, which drives it to the extent of shouting and even violence. And of course, the ego loves to complain and blame others because you are right; your ego tells you so. There is nothing that strengthens the ego more than being right and it feeds directly into the self-worth we crave.

Imagine if we let go of egos and would enter every discussion with a completely open mind, simply looking to discuss facts? Now that would be productive, wouldn't it? Unfortunately, this is rare as every ego is a master of selective perception and distorted interpretation. By now, you're probably thinking of ego-centric managers you have met. Great leaders, on the other hand, cannot afford an ego because it will distract them from fulfilling their purpose.

A person with an ego will usually play a 'role' if they want something from someone else. People doing this are unaware they're doing it at all, their ego controls their subconscious, and eventually these people become the role they play. They end up losing their authenticity, and as a consequence, we do not trust them and will not follow their lead.

Let's review some of the people I described from my own working life. You remember the discussion about the Amex commercial and whether the actors were Europeans or not? Recall that the New York HQ still had to approve the final version. Well that was many egos at play and it was a waste of time. When I worked for the insurance company, the CEO wanted to make all decisions. His ego fueled him fears which he unconsciously reacted to. How about the head of the international division in Fidelity? He was a very insecure person whose ego needed strengthening by intimidating everyone around him. Ned Johnson, on the other hand, never showed an ego, was open for new ideas, and did not insist on making the decisions. He just wanted to see Fidelity succeed and placed the company's success over his own. With Credit Suisse, I wouldn't even know where to start. There were no great leaders but an executive board with bigger egos than anything I've ever seen.

In today's discussions, in politics, in the office, or just at a dinner, people take sides quite quickly. He is right and she is wrong, or vice versa. Look at the dinner discussions about Trump. People are either for him or against him. Those against him will rattle off a long list of reasons why Trump is simply the worst. Those for him will do the opposite. And the dinner? Well, that will be spoiled by egos trying to win. The ego will not necessarily really pay attention to any argument, nor try to understand them. However, it will continuously work to come up with more arguments why it's right. When two sides engage in that manner, it becomes pointless, frustrating and people often succumb to name calling and even raising their voices. It does not have to be like that though. We could have great discussions where everybody would be interested in listening to the other's contribution in hopes of finding a better solution – a far cry from simply taking sides and trying to win.

I find it sad but funny that a man – who wakes up next to his wife who starts bitching at him, then sits exactly the same way on a toilet with his pants around his ankles – looking as stupid as anyone else totally changes once he enters the office in a suit and tie, doing anything he can to live up to the role described on his business card. Everybody in the office will treat him like he is special, they will open the door for him, tell him his ideas are great, and laugh at his stupid jokes. One morning, he will wake up thinking, 'Hey, I am a very important person!' expecting everyone should treat him like that.

I have the pleasure of knowing one of Germany's former most celebrated CEOs and he once openly shared his downfall. He said this downfall changed his life and attitude. He openly shared how he had behaved as a celebrated CEO, for example showing up to important events but leaving if he did not have the most important seat. When I met him, he was a changed man that could openly speak about his ridiculous behavior in his former life – very refreshing.

As said earlier, if our ego forces us to believe we are what we have (titles or things), we will always seek more. That's why every manager wants to be promoted, either to get a bit more power, or a higher salary to buy more things, that again makes him or her feel they are better than others. So, it's an endless game of 'mine is bigger than yours' and that certainly cannot be productive. So as long as people are not fulfilled in their own being but need their ego to constantly fulfil them, we will have assholes and managers. And this goes on in politics as well as business. But it is important for us to be aware of this if we are going to change things for the better. Because ego centric people are unlikely to solve the worlds issues and especially the divide between rich and poor. They actually thrive on it.

One other point about the four leaders described; they all showed early signs of uniqueness and leadership. I would argue they were born to lead, and that we will always have people with the capacity to be leaders among us. I do not believe you can learn to be a great leader but with a clear purpose or passion you might learn to set your ego aside.

So, let's conclude that it is more likely than not that great leaders are born as such and that the core leadership traits are: a strong purpose overriding their own ego; great communication skills, allowing a following to emerge; and a rennetless pursuit to achieve their purpose or vision. Now compare that with most managers and CEOs you know or see. I believe they are a far cry from that. And for the real assholes, well forgive them, they are simply unconscious about how they are being played by their ego. They are of course destructive and we must get rid of them or at least reduce them in numbers, which I will allude to in the last section of the book. But for now, let's just be glad we realize the power and importance of great leaders and move on to look at the challenges and purposes that we, with their leadership, must address.

# PART III

# TECHNOLOGY AND LEADERSHIP CHALLENGES

# 19.
# WEALTH AND INCOME INEQUALITY

At any given time in world history, the human race has been confronted with issues or challenges that can change how we live, and no other factor has changed our way of living more than technology. One of the first and most important technologies invented was the printing press. It allowed knowledge and information to be shared, and when you share knowledge that accelerates progress. For example, I might read a book from a French inventor and perhaps take his idea a step further. It was a revolution that would have a profound impact on future developments, innovations, and, obviously, education. Of course, as it was invented in a time where most world order was underpinned by religion, it was not equally welcomed in all places. People could inform themselves in other ways and through that, form an opinion or even worse, decide what was right or wrong. The printing press was banned by the clergy under the Ottoman Empire as it was partly seen as a threat to the authority of the ruling religious leaders. My fellow Dane Lars Tvede writes in his book *The Creative Society* about how this held back progress and development there versus the rest of the world, evident even today. Around 1880, electric power supply began to revolutionize everything, from how we lived to how we worked. Shortly after we got the telephone and then the radio, which allowed direct communication to the masses, and this was used and abused by politicians influencing world events. The engine and the industrial revolution changed how we worked and the tools we used. Masses of people were no longer needed in the fields and modern efficiencies developed in most daily undertakings, like transportation or washing clothes, which gave way to new and unthinkable life styles. TV amplified the impact radio had had, and often it became the center of family life – in the Western world, that is. Suddenly, it was possible to gain information in both words and pictures, directly into your living room, from all over the world! We embraced new technologies and entered a steady, enduring phase of growth in which most people's lives improved. The Internet was a further revolution in itself; that, combined with the smart phone, drastically changed most things around how we work, communicate, and live. Technology, science, and global trade had a tremendous impact on the world's development and achieved a standard never seen before in terms of the poverty and literacy rate, as well as life expectancy.

In 1990, 36% of the world population lived on less than $1.9 a day. Today it is 10%, with 41% of them found in Sub-Saharan Africa. The official poverty rate has fallen to a historic low of 12.3%. At the same time, health has improved as some of the worst epidemics have been cured, and, as a result, the child mortality rate had fallen 99% between 1900 and 1997.[1] In 1950, there were 59 countries where one out of five children died; today there are none, although Africa and Afghanistan still have a relatively high child mortality rate. Life expectancy has increased from 50 to 80 years in the last century, and a child born in the Western world today can expect to live well over 100 years. At the same time, literacy rates have improved tremendously. In 1820, the global literacy rate was 12%, in 1960 it had grown to 42%, and in 2015 it was 86%. This is a major coup for education and people's ability to inform themselves. So again, science, technology, and global trade has given us an amazing world, but, though this is obviously fantastic, there are two drastic issues.

Firstly, despite the global boost in wealth, income and wealth distribution has deteriorated. It's measured by the Gini coefficient which measures income inequality, where 0 is full income equality and 100 is the highest possible inequality. Not surprisingly, Scandinavian countries like Norway and Sweden have one of the lowest in the world, around 25; a number of corrupt African countries scored highest, around 65. According to the Gini coefficient, income inequality has grown since 1970 to new highs.

The world's GDP has gone from $695 billion in 1820 to $87 trillion in 2018. In 1820, Western Europe accounted for roughly 23% of the world's GDP, and the US accounted for less than 2%, so all together less than 25% according to economist Angus Maddison. In the same year, China accounted for 27%, more than Europe and the US together. In 1950, Europe had grown to account for 28% and the US around 4.5% so together around a third, while China had fallen, accounting for only 4.5%. In 2008, Western Europe and the US combined to a rough total of 37% and for China it was 17.5%. That means Western Europe (14 countries), the US, and China accounted for 53.5% of the world's GDP. It is astonishing to see China's economic development shuffle back and forth, from rich to poor and back to rich, and the US and Europe growing from poor to rich. What should be remembered, today Europe accounts for only 5.3% of the world's population and the US for 4.3%, meaning 9.6% of the world's population accounts for 37% of the GDP. China on the other hand accounts for 18.5% of the world's population and around the same share of the GDP. In sharp contrast to this stands Africa, which in 2008 accounted for 3% of the world's GDP and 16% of the world's population. Through viewing the countries and their populations, we see a very unequal distribution of wealth. An added note: Africa is not poor; it is simply poorly managed through corrupt officials accepting bribes from foreign countries and firms in exchange for African assets. Countries like Holland and Denmark, the least corrupt countries, became very wealthy, despite their lack of natural resources.

Secondly, income and wealth inequality stand to significantly deteriorate due to a new technology push including in, among others,

AI and Blockchain. In the late 20th century, computers and the Internet, followed by smart phones, gave a substantial boost to productivity and wealth creation, again transforming how we work and the tools we use. The Internet helped with the spread of access to information and catered to a new entrepreneurial boom. Throughout the 20th century, the world largest firms have always been those in the oil business, banks, and car manufactures, and they were well established, long-running enterprises. Today, the top ten highest valued firms in the world are relatively new technology firms like Amazon, Apple, Google, and Facebook. Only two 'traditional' firms make it to the top 10: Exxon and J.P Morgan. Astounding, but it points to a very clear trend. The most valuable car company at the time of writing is Tesla, which is less than 15-years-old. Wealth has increased tremendously for those who started these businesses. Bill Gates (Microsoft), Marc Zuckerberg (Facebook), Jeff Bezos (Amazon), Larry Page and Sergey Brin (Google) are all among the 10 wealthiest people in the world, having amassed unthinkable fortunes in an incredibly short time span. In fact, the 26 richest people today own the same as the poorest 50% of the entire human race, which is close to 4 billion people, according to Oxfam's newest report.[2] Let me repeat that: The 26 richest people today own the same as the poorest 50% of the entire human race, which is close to 4 billion people. The number of billionaires has doubled in the last decade to around 2,700 people, since the 2008 financial crisis. In 2018 alone, the wealth of billionaires increased by around $2 billion every single day: an average of roughly $750,000 per billionaire. In addition, a new person becomes a billionaire every second day.[3] By contrast, the poorest 50% in the world have to survive on an average of $5 per day. If we look at Fortune 500 CEOs, they make roughly 204 times more than their average worker. That's 20 times more than it was in 1950. Have CEOs become that much better in the last 68 years or just greedier?

Thomas Piketty, who I will return to later in the book, made an analysis of this subject. His findings were what I expected – there have been no noticeable increases in the productivity of CEOs over employees. He puts high executive pay down to luck, meaning increases in executive earnings are not related to talent, nor related to a reward for good performance. He describes the *luck factor* to be said executives' abilities to demand or negotiate substantial pay packages, and that too is not clearly justified by their economic performance. Interestingly, in countries with lower income taxes, the pay packages are relatively higher, explained by a higher incentive to negotiate harder as the marginal return is greater. A good example of this is Switzerland. The argument that competition for talented executives drove executive pay higher could not be substantiated in his research. My own experiences and observations can easily confirm these findings. I was totally overpaid in Credit Suisse, and there were several people in the organization that could have done my job and for a significantly lower pay package. Look at the pay packages of large companies running huge yearly losses, and look at companies whose shareholders are suffering but executives are paid grand bonuses to make up for their loss in their shares or options. I have seen it all and I'm convinced that most highly paid executives are simply lucky. I certainly could not believe my own luck when I was presented with my pay package at Credit Suisse!

Before we go on, let's look at why income inequality is a problem. Well, have you travelled to South America lately? I go there often, and I love the place and its people, having made many friends there. It so happens that they are all very well off but they're in the minority. They are surrounded by security 24/7, drive armored cars, have private security guards, bullet proof windows, alarm systems, and huge fences around their homes. Their kids have no freedom to be kids. When I tell them my daughter was running around freely in our neighborhood in Switzerland at the age of five, they don't believe me. The sad fact is a nice T-shirt is worth more than a human life when differences are too drastic and the poor simply try to survive. At my last dinner party in Venezuela, usually among a larger crowd, not a single guest was free of the shadow of kidnapped or slain family members – a situation born out of inequality.

In Europe, we have seen an influx of poor immigrants, especially over the last few years. If that were me and my family, if we had no choice but to migrate from Africa, if it was a matter of feeding my family, I would swim or sail over any ocean and steal your car if that's what it took. These are basic observations but a World Bank study confirmed strong correlations between inequality and crime, both within a society but also between countries.[4] Inequality has a broader impact than just fueling crime. According to Organisation for Economic Co-operation and Development (OECD), it negatively impacts trust in the society, fuels social unrest and political volatility, creates health issues, as well as hinders economic growth – especially in countries with high inequality. It should be noted that most economists argue inequality is a good thing, if not a necessity. But we are talking about inequality that has increased to levels unheard of, which raises the serious question if this has spiraled out of control? Is it sustainable to keep it at this level, never mind letting it rise further? This is mainly debated by economists throwing around jargon related to economic growth and there might not be clear answers. Logic would dictate that economic growth would give the poor a better chance of getting a job but, as I mentioned, it's not clear whether a very high level of inequality spurs growth. In fact, a study by OECD found that in the US when inequality goes beyond a certain point, a Gini coefficient higher than 27, (it is currently 41) it negatively impacts growth. It is estimated that from 1990 to 2010, a period of rising inequality in the US knocked 5% off the cumulative GDP per capita.

Although these are important facts, we need to question economic growth as an overriding goal and solution to most economic issues. Do the very poor worry about economic growth as such? They just want to eat. The monetary system is interest-based and debt is often used to spur economic (paper) growth. But with debt, seen most recently in 2008, comes enormous risks: unemployment, lowering wages, reduced government services, or outright bankruptcy. All of these lead to a greater gap between the wealthy and the poor. GDP only tells us how much economic activity is happening, not how the wealth is generated (is it through destructive activities?). It also does not tell us where the wealth flows (maybe right out of the country a year later?). Some of Trump's current policies, such as lowering taxes, limiting health care, building oil pipelines in Alaska are all done in the name of economic growth. Obviously, growth in itself is a very good thing, but to look at every political decision from a growth perspective is simply wrong.

The OECD, along with the International Monetary Fund and the World Bank, are increasingly sounding the alarm bells that growing inequality is hurting everyone, independent of economic status. The well-to-do are borne through an educated workforce and a broad consumer base, both of which decline through higher levels of inequality. Furthermore, we have witnessed throughout history that when a large demographic feels like they're left behind, they will do whatever they can to change it. That being revolution, war, unrest, or simply voting for stupid populist politicians, who will drag inequality down although will likely make everybody poorer. This is the key concern: when a large part of the population feels left behind, left out or even cheated, populists can flourish. Politicians with little experience or competence grab a chance to feed on the inequality with simple messages, in most cases with a single focus to distribute income. All over the world, we have seen this taking place, and it typically leaves a country worse off. Look at some African countries, like Zimbabwe run by former president Robert Mugabe. Look at Venezuela today, a country that stands as one with the poorest population and highest crime rate. Their president? A former bus driver with populist messages. Venezuela used to be one of the richest countries in the world with a large middle class, but voters were made stupid promises, like that they will receive a house from the government. Since that might be their only chance to get a house, they vote accordingly. But populists can also drive the other way. Partly elected by the lower, uneducated middle class, Donald Trump gave major tax cuts to the rich along with little change for the poor. The argument here is the trickle-down effect, which raises the question: if the wealthy people become wealthier, will they spend and invest in jobs? Unfortunately, there is no clear answer here either. That trickle-down effect does exist but when the 26 richest people (who already have more wealth than the 4 billion poorest) get richer, will there still be a trickle-down effect? Would it have been better to give some of their money directly to the poorer demographic? Well, only history can judge Trump's tax cut as making sense or not, but there are plenty of reasons to be skeptical.

Along with high inequality, populists also appoint an enemy to blame. With Trump, it's immigrants: they're stealing jobs; they're increasing the crime rate; heck, they killed Santa Claus too. His answer to this claim, which he deemed a national emergency, is to build the famous, tall, beautiful wall (or fence depending what day you ask him). The reason is so simple that even the dumbest person can understand it: Immigrants walk over the border, if there is a wall then they cannot and we have solved the issue. This simple message helped him become president, the leader of the free world. Why? Sixty million people felt left out and that's all it took. We have more than half the world's population left behind; this is not sustainable and poses a huge risk to our global society. If we acknowledge that we have reached this intolerable level of inequality then we need to act now, especially since new technologies stand to eliminate multiple job categories, potentially increasing inequality even further.

Let's take a closer look at those technologies to understand what we should expect and what issues we might have to deal with. The two technologies I explore are Blockchain and Artificial Intelligence. Both are great innovations that will impact our lives, and both come with great risks as well as opportunities.

# 20.
# THE PROMISE OF
# BLOCKCHAIN

Blockchain was everywhere in 2018, but understood by few to none. Let's first understand the basics of the technology and then go into the application of it.

The basis of Blockchain is Distributed Ledger Technology (DLT). A 'ledger' is simply a stored record or filing. 'Distributed' simply indicates you store the same information in multiple places. In essence, instead of only one computer 'holding' the fact that you are the rightful owner of, say, a certain house, hundreds or thousands or even millions of computers now store that fact. The result is a high degree of safety for that given fact. In essence, it's impossible to hack hundreds of thousands of computers at the same time to 'steal' or change the data. If hundreds of computers all hold the fact that you are the owner of that house, then you are. That is, in very basic terms, what DLT offers and the basis of Blockchain (it should be noted that the Bitcoins that have been 'stolen', something that is often brought up, have not been stolen from the bitcoin Blockchain but from a trading exchange). The word Blockchain stems from the process of securely storing transaction data on multiple computers. Let's say 10 people all bought a Bitcoin; these 10 transactions are 'blocked', meaning put into a combined block. 'Chain' indicates that this block will be chained to the latest stored block (the last transaction securely stored) in one move to the entire network, creating a chain of transactions. The actual way this is done caters to the correctness and security of the transaction through a 'mining' process, which is a highly complicated mathematical challenge that needs to be solved before the 'block' can be stored or filed on the Blockchain network. Special 'miners', which are actually people solving these mathematical challenges, take care of this and are rewarded financially for doing so. Unfortunately, it's so complicated that mining Bitcoin uses the same energy as all of Australia together – not eco-friendly at all and certainly not scalable.

The way to think about Blockchain is simply a safe, immutable storage of a fact on maybe millions of computers (the Blockchain network) with proof of transaction history through the blocks. That's it. Although the concept has been around for a long time, it was really harnessed by the inventors of Bitcoin to enable a 'free' currency for a libertarian world. Bitcoin itself is simply a cryptocurrency, an alternative investment product, and nothing else. Like all other cryptocurrencies, there is no real value behind it save what a person is willing to pay for it. Given that cryptocurrencies are unregulated, highly speculative and volatile, and, in my opinion, irrelevant in their current form, I will not go deeper into them but focus on the Blockchain technology behind it.

Now that we have a technology that can guarantee safe, un-hackable storage of data and transactions, what possibilities does that open? Well, the short answer is *everything*. The promise of Blockchain is that it might actually deliver where the Internet has fallen short, mainly due to failed politics and regulations. The Internet promised to democratize businesses, allowing anyone to build a business relatively easily and take on existing players. Although that held true in the beginning, it does not any longer. Today we realize the Internet has built monopolies on a scale unseen before: Google, Amazon, Facebook, and Uber, to mention a few. You cannot start a business on the Internet and acquire clients without making companies like Google and Facebook bigger and richer before making any money yourself. The Internet also set out to ensure we could engage in a digitalized society, and once upon a time that might have been true. Today though, you do not know if a person portrays their real name, real picture, real address, or if it's even a real person, so there can be little to no trust. The Internet was supposed to bank the 'unbankable' and those left behind in the economy. In certain instances it has but not nearly on the scale hoped for. The Internet allowed digital money transfer and payments but the fact is your bank account can be hacked. I personally only buy half of what I would like to on the Internet as I am somewhat anxious about where my money will actually go and if I will ever get the product. Or perhaps that vacation house I rented doesn't actually exist or is owned by someone else. The Internet has been fantastic in providing us information. We can access *any* information from *anywhere* at *any time*. We don't need to retain information these days – it's all there. This has killed a lot of otherwise good dinner conversations as there is always a person that immediately Googles the facts and brings the discussion to an end. Great as it is, the fact remains that the Internet is a totally untrustworthy platform that has reached its limits for substantial progress. It has served its purpose as the Internet of **Information** extremely well, but we now need a trusted platform for the next generation: the Internet of **Value**. And that is where Blockchain comes into the picture, assuming it can integrate the processes in an easy way and bring the required governance and regulation behind it.

This innovative technology, described in very basic terms above, is set to revolutionize most things we deal with today. I do not use the word revolutionize by coincidence. When I started to get involved in Blockchain myself, I decided to read a book by Don and Alex Tapscott, *Blockchain Revolution*. I believe that any book you read today on Blockchain is outdated as everything develops so fast, but that book is still legendary despite being written in 2015. As the book helped me shape my views, as well as inspired me to get more involved with Blockchain, I will have to give a lot of credit to the Tapscott brothers and proudly present some of their views alongside my own.

The trust that can be assumed in a Blockchain network allows peer-to-peer transactions. I believe that one day most of us will have our 'trusted' identities registered on a Blockchain platform. Imagine you 'meet' me on the Internet. As mentioned before, you do not know if any of the information is real or fake. You are careful with your own data because you do not own it and companies like Google and Facebook 'steal' your personal data, selling it for a lump sum. On Blockchain, your personal information is yours and nobody can access it unless you decide to release the information. Let's assume we 'meet' on a Blockchain platform. You will see I make certain claims around my identity, such as my nationality, address, that I have cleared a financial KYC (Know Your Clients done by banks today to ensure you are who you are and that you are not a crook), that I have a Visa for the US. You cannot see my individual data but what you will see is that the data I claim to have is endorsed. Using myself as an example, you will see that my passport is endorsed by the Danish Government, my address by the Zurich Residential Registry, my Visa by US Immigration Services, my KYC by UBS bank. I can build my identity with as many claims as I wish and you can see endorsement of these claims. As this information is on Blockchain, no one can hack or change it and we can now start to 'trust' each other and stay away from those without endorsements. You might also hold all your health data and medical records in your Blockchain identity to ensure that if you are in a hospital, you can release the data and your doctor can get full access in seconds. This is private data that you own and no one else has access to, unless you allow them permission. You might decide to let some of it be seen by insurance firms in the hope of getting a better insurance offer or you might get paid for your information. The point is you control your information. This will make Facebook and Co. irrelevant as the businesses they are today, but they will most likely find a way to adapt.

Blockchain allows us to endow our digital identity as a secured and trusted asset. It is a persistent digital identity on to which you can keep adding claims and endorsements, according to your needs for different relationships or transactions. It allows your 'reputation' to be used in social and economic systems, without having to prove yourself every time. Blockchain allows the building of a trusted society or, should we say, a society where we actually do not need trust, just facts. This is huge considering the problems of society today. This does not, in any way, lead directly to a re-distribution of wealth but, maybe more importantly, to a wider distribution of opportunity that will affect income distribution in a positive way.

Having your secured digital identity on the Blockchain platform, it would be logical to secure your assets, the things you own, under that same identity. You might, with the help of endorsements or digitalized documents, put your car, your house, your investments, your Picasso painting etc. under your identity. To do so, those assets must be digitalized or tokenized. You may, for example, 'tokenize' your Picasso painting into, say, one or 100 tokens. Whoever owns those digitalized tokens, each representing an underlying value such as a house or painting, has a financial right to the future economics of that asset. If I have one token out of the 100 tokens in your Picasso painting, I own 1% of that painting and when you sell it, I will receive 1% of the sale price directly from the buyer. With tokenization, each form of asset will have their own identity but represented and split into tokens. These tokens, demonstrating clear ownership of digitalized assets, can be locked to an identity, so you and I can now transfer, exchange, or pay with those tokens. That's called the Internet of **Value**, a platform where we trust each other and therefore transfer, pay with, or exchange assets.

The interesting part is we can do this without any intermediary. We do not need a bank, a real estate broker, a platform like Airbnb, or any middleman to bridge the trust gap. We can do everything peer-to-peer. I buy your car with my one token in a Picasso painting and the transaction will settle and be locked safely on the Blockchain, where ownership of your car will be transferred in the same instant that my token transfers to you. The Tapscott brothers described it as follows:

'We can each own our own identities and our personal data. We can do transactions, creating and exchanging value without powerful intermediaries acting as the arbiters of money and information. Billions of excluded people can soon enter the global economy. We can protect our privacy and monetize our own information. We can ensure that creators are compensated for their intellectual property. Rather than trying to solve the problem of growing social inequality through the redistribution of wealth alone, we can start to change the way wealth is distributed – how it is created in the first place, as people everywhere from farmers to musicians can share more fully, a priori, in the wealth they create.'

In essence what they argue is that where new technologies mostly automate peoples work, Blockchain can ensure people benefit directly from the value they create. For the sharing economy, Airbnb, Uber, and more will no longer be needed as a trust and settlement platform between parties. Blockchain does not put the Uber driver out of work, it puts Uber out of work and allows the drivers to work directly with passengers. The financial world has been a bastion for interruptions by new technologies and remains one of the most inefficient industries with endless expensive settlement procedures through multiple intermediaries (who make great fees). The high costs that this results in can now be eliminated by Blockchain as the financial industry will be revolutionized with peer-to-peer transaction possibilities. This also means the unbankable demographic can now be connected and included in financial activity. This further liberation of entrepreneurship will have a profound impact on fighting inequality. The management of property rights on Blockchain will give a further boost to fighting inequality as they are the essence of economic opportunity. Unfortunately, in many developing countries, property right is a difficult thing to prove as it's often poorly recorded and ripe for fraud and corruption. The fact that people can now prove their ownership of a piece of land, a property, a car, or a specific right for the use of land on Blockchain will fuel economic opportunity for them.

It goes a step further: I recently had a meeting with the former Prime Minister of an Eastern European country (one of those where it's predictable who will be the next President and that was him). What he said delighted me and gave me hope. He started out stating the key issues his country faced. Firstly, tremendous corruption when, as an example, the capital transfers money to a remote village only 50% arrives. Secondly, collecting taxes. And thirdly, collecting sales tax. He explained how the sale of an iPhone resulted in a sales tax of $30 when it should have been $120. He explained that these three factors alone held back any economic and social progress of the country, and he wanted to solve that. Ironically, in the entourage he brought with him was also the wealthiest businessman in the country, who seemed wholeheartedly to support this goal. When I asked how they would succeed in doing this, the former Prime Minister blurted out, 'With Blockchain, of course'. He then went to a smart board and drew and talked for 30 minutes, explaining how Blockchain would eradicate corruption and ensure collection of all taxes. I have seen a lot in my life, but this must rate as one of the most impressive things I have experienced. His country has a resident register, a tax register, a health register, a housing register, and a car register. But they are not matched, merged, or purged. With Blockchain, he envisaged he would have one register with residents including their assets, like house and car etc. This is the brave new world with government transparency. If the police stop a guy driving a Lamborghini, but he hasn't paid his taxes or got documentation proving clear ownership of the car then the car is gone – as simple as that. When money is sent from the capital directly to the account of the remote villages, there would be high security and full transparency on every cent. How that money is spent, every single transfer, would be fully transparent. And voila, a big chunk of corruption disappears. The result he's looking for is to move his country into the top 10 least corrupt countries in the world, as well as to have a flourishing economy, benefiting the broader population.

In my banking career, I have met so many self-serving, greedy, corrupt individuals so this was refreshing. If his country can do it, so can others. Blockchain stands to transform governments and countries on a scale never seen before, assuming of course they have great leaders. Hernando de Soto, a leading economic mind, estimates that as many as five billion people in the world are barred from participating fully in economic value development because of tenuous right to their land. A rightful registration of property and land rights will allow for basic things, like obtaining a loan, get building permits, or selling the property, and ensuring that it cannot be expropriated by corrupt officials. Blockchain will support a new agenda of global justice and economic growth for the forgotten demographic.

Ownership and rights stand to have further profound impacts on inequality, not through wealth distribution but through the original source where the value was created. Take artistic rights where the industry of music, art, photography, etc. will be revolutionized. Music owners do not know what percentage of what royalties they should get, and most likely are underpaid today. That will change with Blockchain as it not only secures their ownership rights but also makes transparent who used their work and what they're owed. The creator (in this case the musician, the photographer, the filmmaker) stands to get a fairer share of their value creation. Blockchain provides the creator the opportunity to cut out the middlemen and leave with more value. With Blockchain, ownership, rights management, and wealth creation will be distributed more fairly than anything today.

There are many more potential positives in fighting inequality through Blockchain technology. Take the area of remittance. The largest flow of funds into a developing country is remittance from people working abroad, sending money home to their families. For some countries, it accounts for 10–20% of their GDP. Remittance sounds simple but is in essence an activity that is cumbersome, sometimes dangerous, and certainly ripe for high fees and even fraud, as both the sender and receiver are not banked, especially with larger institutions. That is not to say larger institutions don't commit fraud, they do – it's unfortunately legalized fraud… Remittance done in 2020 can easily take a week and costs up to 20%. For receivers in the Philippines alone, this is a loss of billions a year in unnecessary transaction fees. With Blockchain, it can cost a fraction and be done within minutes. It will kill intermediaries, and the people desperately in need of the money stand to win.

There is also foreign aid and charity. As described in an earlier chapter, my wife set up and runs our charity called Future4Children, which exposed us to the world of collecting, sending, and spending charity money. In collecting charity money, very wealthy people do not give to charity because they are worried about the potential inefficiency of a charity organization and fear that maybe only 50% of their donation actually goes to help those in need. The topic deserves a book of its own as it's a destructive concern or simply a bad excuse. Firstly, even if only 50% were actually given directly to those in need, that would have a life changing effect on said recipients. Rather than worry about the 50% being used inefficiently, worry about the impact the remaining 50% will bring. With Blockchain and full transparency of every dime, that excuse would disappear and significantly more charitable funds could be collected. Then there is also the sending of money, especially with foreign aid, where money and goods simply disappear in a chain of corrupt and incompetent politicians and officials. Blockchain would lay this bare, and through that transparency make corruption in terms of stealing impossible. Equally important is how said funds are spent, this would also be transparent and spent according to the promised agreements verified on the smart contract. In essence, donors could track every cent of their donation, increasing the efficiency standing of foreign aid and charity. By ensuring the wealthy give more, the poor get more and corrupt officials get less; in this way Blockchain would again address inequality.

Entrepreneurship is an important driver of economic development for any country. It is especially important for developing countries where the younger generations face great difficulty in finding steady employment. As we have seen around the world, young restless men, without a job or purpose, engage in destructive activities, such as crime or terrorism. You could argue that Robin Hood-like crime addresses economic inequality, but this is the worst 'solution', as everybody stands to lose in the longer run. The Internet once gave hope that spurred entrepreneurship around the world, sadly global entrepreneurship has been declining during the last 30 years. Tapscott argues that Blockchain will spur entrepreneurship in at least three ways. Firstly, with trusted identities and company record keeping, the formation of a company should be easier. In some developing countries the formation phase can include multiple permissions from incompetent officials and therefore take six to 12 months. With Blockchain it could be done in a fraction of that time and at a fraction of the cost. Secondly, the funding of a company is obviously a major stumbling block for entrepreneurs. But with Blockchain, people can easily prove their assets and obtain loans or simply access a trusted global capital market with their digital identity, perhaps obtaining financing. Thirdly, access to buyers based on a trusted global platform, is enabled. The buyer will not need a credit card anymore. In addition, the running of the business, record keeping, accounting etc. is set to be significantly easier and cheaper as the need for advisors, such as lawyers and accountants, will be reduced. As for the business itself? It can be anything from renting out your kitchen or goat to... well, the sky is the limit with trusted peer-to-peer enabled transactions. This unleashing of entrepreneurship for the masses and the forgotten will address inequality, as people around the world are enabled to create value for themselves.

Blockchain can also support democracy. Well, in these times, democracy is a questionable system. Democracy elected Trump and other populist leaders set up Britain for Brexit and elected Maduro, now a dictator ruining Venezuela. How did that happen? Well, democracy builds on a well-informed, engaged middle class. In today's world where people inform themselves through the Internet, they know everything about the Kardashians, but they cannot find their own country on a map. The middle class is eroding in countries, such as the US and conspiracy theories are enforced through the Internet. I believe we have reached the limits of democracy; it does not work as well as it used to.

Targeted communication through big data algorithms has allowed enemies of the state, or extremists and ideologists, to not only highjack the political debate, but also to mislead, manipulate, and create fake news, influencing public opinion and elections. The Internet has become a place of taking sides rather than having informed debates. As Tapscott writes, the Web can further ignorance and denialism to the degree it outguns scientists and rationalists. Democracy is under attack and that should wake us up. All this is said well knowing that democracy has only proven to be relatively better than say socialism, communism, and dictatorship. Regardless of your personal favorite, we should have a fact-based, unemotional discussion about what is the best political system going forward. Is it democracy where politicians must qualify by showing real competence? Should a Minister of Finance not have some economic background and financial knowledge before being able to be elected as such? Should voters be qualified and show they have a minimum understanding of the problems facing their nation? Can Blockchain save democracy and actually make it work as intended? How? First of all, it can help make elections fair. Today, in many emerging countries, and in the US according to Trump, elections are manipulated to generate desired outcomes for those holding the power. Blockchain can solve that through a clear voter registry and digital voting. Secondly, people might be more encouraged to vote if they can vote with one click, rather than take a day off to go to a polling station. Given that more of the population will vote maybe they will inform themselves a little more, leading to increasing engagement. Thirdly, the influence of fake news and conspiracy theory would significantly decline and perhaps encourage people to participate, should facts be easier to obtain. Blockchain can also enable what is currently called a liquid democracy or delegative democracy. It allows citizens to customize their democratic voting right as the idea is that they can delegate voting authority to multiple representatives across an array of topics. In 2020, I live in the world's most democratic country, Switzerland. Almost every important vote is put to a referendum, either in the state or the nation. The problem with that is the very idea of democracy: that you elect the politician you most believe in to represent you. It is his or her full-time job to understand the issues and help decide on issues you cannot or do not have time to understand and vote on. Blockchain, in essence, could easily allow a referendum on any issue, but I hope it will not get to that. Let's try to save and improve democracy according to the model that has served the developing world well in the last decades. So, great political leaders must push for technology solutions and think through how best to apply them because in the end, Blockchain is just a technology.

Blockchain, particularly in combination with other new technologies such as Artificial Intelligence, stands to revolutionize almost all aspects of our lives and in so doing, has a huge potential to address inequality. It also stands to introduce efficiencies that the Internet could not and the impact on job losses (not to mention entire job categories) will be huge. The good news is that it can eliminate inefficient ego-driven managers and corrupt politicians, referred to as the assholes in the title of this book.

At business school you learn about 'agency cost' which describes the cost of misalignment between owners and the firm. In other words, it's the costly inefficiency of bureaucracy, hierarchy, and politics applied by managers in orchestrating and coordinating the firm's activities to create value. Costs increase because managers stand between the leader (or leaders) and the workers or sales people, and the managers allocate resources via authoritative directions, often based on ignorant assumptions as well as their ego, of course. Very rarely are their decisions fully fact-based. Tapscott states that over the last few decades, hierarchies have come under scrutiny as structures for killing creativity, undermining initiative, disempowering human capital, and scapegoating responsibility through opacity. This is fully aligned with my own experience. I do not recall a situation where a major mistake caused by management was acknowledged and taken responsibility for by a manager. When something goes wrong, a scapegoat far down the organization is blamed and let go, not the manager causing the mistake. The Internet has helped somewhat in helping firms achieve internal collaboration, but it has failed in true empowerment of the ground people, the people actually doing the job and creating value. Unfortunately, this 'gap' between the leader and the ground people produces a huge inefficiency, namely agency cost. So how will Blockchain impact this? Well, in a good many ways.

Blockchain can produce transparency and can do so throughout a firm's organization. It can store facts on a massive scale that can serve for a full 'run through' of all activities from the very top, and allow sensible fact-based decisions to be taken. It might actually be the end of the PowerPoint presentation culture! Through smart contracts, a core essence of Blockchain, agency cost at all levels of management can be reduced. So, imagine full transparency for operating procedures, where performance is guided or 'managed' through smart contracts rather than ego centric managers. This can ensure directions leaders want are not misinterpreted or diluted through a hierarchy down to the front line. In essence, we can get rid of the hierarchy. Even shareholders can easily follow the company performance in detail, a very scary thing for managers. Remember, the definition of agency cost: misalignment of managers and owners. Well, Blockchain will force alignment, mainly by making managers largely obsolete as they are only intermediaries – exactly what Blockchain can get rid of. With Blockchain, leaders can easily distribute responsibility, authority, and power, which will improve a firm's performance and perhaps foster innovation.

So, from the above examples, it should be clear that Blockchain stands to make profound changes, some of which will enable a better world and many of which will directly address the inequality problem. But as it will also potentially cut out all middle-men and trust building businesses, jobs are at risk on a large scale. We will now add Artificial Intelligent and its impact to the mix, and things will get really exciting!

# 21.
# ARTIFICIAL INTELLIGENCE AND JOBS

The term Artificial Intelligence (AI), first coined by a Stanford researcher back in 1956, is one of the hottest and most debated buzz words today. Depending on who you listen to, it's either an amazing new technology or the end of humankind. So, we're in the relatively early stages where it can go both ways and now is the time to reflect on its impact on greater society, especially inequality. Before getting into any reflections, let's take a quick look at the technology.

The researcher, John McCarty, stated AI is 'The science and engineering of making intelligent machines, especially intelligent computer programs'. But what does intelligent mean in this context? It means building technology (computers and software) capable of **thinking**, **acting** and **learning** like humans. Sound scary? Could be. My first encounter with the idea of AI was in 1983 watching the movie *War Games*, in which an intelligent computer takes control of the Pentagon and starts to plan, initiate, and conduct a nuclear war. Is that realistic though? In my opinion, very much so. Essentially, AI is based on massive pools of data that is analyzed and used to reach conclusions, recommendations, or actions. In *War Games*, the computer played a full game of action and reaction, constantly adjusting and adapting in order to beat the enemy. To achieve this at a high level requires huge data sets and machine learning. Often machine learning and AI are used interchangeably but they are *not* the same thing. Machine learning is based on advanced machines learning from analyzing huge data sets to identify patterns, it's a narrower definition. Whereas AI is a broader concept but still mostly dependent on machine learning. Where have you experienced AI? The easiest example I can think of is playing chess against a computer where the computer 'thinks' of, and analyzes an infinite number of possibilities and combinations going forward. When IBM's Deep Blue computer defeated Garry Kasparov, the world's best chess player, that was a truly significant moment. But more significant, in 2017 Google's AlphaZero program defeated Stockfish 8. AlphaZero utilized AI to *self-learn* how to play chess; Stockfish 8 was the world's chess champion with access to endless years of *human* and computer experience in chess. That the self-learning machine won is incredible.

Language and writing have progressed beyond traditional speaking and writing. From the auto-suggest tool while typing on your smart phone to automatic translation on an app, your computer is 'making sense' of your words when you speak to it. Siri and Alexa, the most popular AI-driven personal assistants today, recognize your speech, understand what you want (some of the time), analyze the information they have access to, and provide an answer or solution – almost like your husband or wife, just without the arguing... They consistently learn about their users so they can better anticipate your needs (an improvement over the husband/wife). Just look at the ads you get in your web browser or on Twitter: tailored to illustrate what an algorithm thinks you are interested in. It might not always be spot on but it's not far off. The same goes for Spotify, Pandora, and Apple music, as well as Amazon, Netflix, and more. We now have a few banks that have started using advisor robots. You might run into a robot trying to have a conversation with you at the airport. AI is very real but we have seen nothing of its full potential yet, and whether we should fear the doomsday scenarios where AI takes over the world from the humans is not that easy to say. My view: in theory yes, in practice no. AI is set to outperform humans in many tasks, such as translation, writing essays, and driving vehicles to name just a few examples. But writing a great book or conducting highly complicated surgery might be a stretch, although I'm sure AI will be integrated in supporting the latter, perhaps even playing the lead role. Would you rather sit in a plane flown by a pilot or AI? Well, we humans make mistakes all the time, and while AI is not perfect, your last plane ride was 90% AI anyway...

All of the above is enabled by big data, endless data that we have great difficulty in analyzing and finding patterns in, to build sensible algorithms that dictate response and action. The more data it has access to, the more AI will outperform humans in certain fields. Just so there is no doubt: big data increases on a daily basis. Each of us pile up (involuntary) data every day through the use of the Internet, walking around with our cell phone, etc. Companies undertake great efforts in collecting data any way they can and big data in itself has become one of the biggest businesses ever. AI can diagnose a patient better than a doctor (straightforward cases), calculate an insurance premium better than an actuary, develop a flight schedule, and determine an optimal building structure to mention a few examples, all based on big data.

From the above description of AI, it should be clear that it will eliminate multiple tasks performed by humans today. Just how big a threat is it really? Well, a large study from McKinsey (a consulting firm) suggests that by 2030 AI and robots could eliminate as much as 30% of today's global human labour.[5] With various scenarios, they reckon 400 to 800 million jobs will be displaced. This is huge and it's only 10 years away! Even with a broader outlook, even the most conservative estimate tells us that jobs will be lost on a scale similar to the industrial revolution away from agricultural labor during the 1900s. The Brookings Institution writes alarmingly of potential consequences where 'The United States would look like Syria or Iraq, with armed bands of young men with few employment prospects other than war, violence, or theft'.[6] At the same time, technology firms like

Uber, Lyft, Slack, Postmates, Pinterest, and Airbnb are all set to enter the public market, turning hypothetical wealth into real wealth, and churning out thousands of multi-millionaires. Sounds like inequality is about to worsen, and potentially, quite dramatically with terrible consequences. Well, that is a negative prediction and I am an optimist, so let's look at some facts and for the opportunities.

As usual, with the arrival of new machines and technologies comes the doomsday scenarios. In 1811, machines were feared regarding the elimination of jobs in the textile industry. A movement called Luddite started, where workers destroyed the machines and burned the factories. Today we know the threat was unfounded. During the last 30 years, it's actually cheaper labor in developing countries that has taken away textile jobs in the developed world. That was good in addressing the inequality issue. Later, it was machines replacing farming and agriculture that was feared. In 1962, President Kennedy stated that 'the major challenge of the sixties is to maintain full employment at a time when automation is replacing men'. Well, a period of tremendous job growth followed where the developed world had to import workers from other countries. In the 1980s, fear of computers set in, predicting a huge loss of employment. We were wrong, again... History has shown that technological development has not killed jobs, rather the opposite. In 1870, around 50% of the population in the US worked in agriculture; in 2008 it was 2% and the country has still managed to prosper, feed its people, and have close to full employment. People migrated from one job to another; from ploughing the land to driving and maintaining a tractor, from sewing to operating and maintaining factory equipment, and so on. The productivity gained in the 19th century in textiles was with a factor of 50 for a given output; only 2% of labor work was needed at the end of the century compared to the beginning, but we survived that.

Will history be an indication of what to expect in the future? A fair question given the dramatic forecasts. Will new jobs be generated on the same scale? That is hard to tell. After all, who could have predicted the smart phone and app developers in 1980? No one I imagine. Instead of speculating on the future, let's identify the type of jobs or tasks that will disappear (we will do this in greater detail in the next chapter). As always, with new technology, it's the less exciting, less rewarding, and more tedious jobs that will go, the physical tasks or mind-numbing jobs. We are potentially freeing up human capacity for something greater, and that is an opportunity we should grab! People can perform their work with a greater sense of meaning and well-being from jobs that challenges them, provides them with autonomy, gives them a sense of impact and all these are factors of higher job satisfaction. Let's assume we migrate people from current tasks to new opportunities; that is a leadership challenge, both in our society and in the companies themselves. We're assuming these are jobs suited for people alone, and that will be the biggest question of all. These technologies aren't disrupting a single industry but virtually all industries and job categories. We will be looking at an acceleration in job elimination, and this will challenge any migration effort in terms of speed and scale. In order to mitigate job losses, education, migration, and development of new job categories will be crucial.

New technologies are also set to help eliminate diseases through great advances in medicine and healthcare. This enables better disease prevention, better diagnosis, and more efficient cures and treatments. As a result, we will live longer. On one hand, this is positive *assuming* there are jobs available for all, but we also risk facing a huge population of older people that need to be taken care of. Who pays for this? Pension systems are already mostly bankrupt; not long ago four people worked for every pensioner in the western world, and very soon it will be one to one, meaning one working person will have to make enough to support themselves plus an extra person. This is a huge challenge to solve. On the other side, the increase in economic activity through technology among the poorer population illustrates the fact that they should be able to pay some of their own way and increase their standard of living. And what about the billionaires-to-be from the new technology? Will they follow Bill Gates' giving pledge or do politicians need to step in?

That's what this comes down to; the challenges for our leaders, politicians, or businesses, are centered around three core issues: education for a new job landscape, managing firms (especially technology firms) with greater focus on social responsibility, and finally political solutions for wealth distribution. Let's look at these three challenges, one by one.

# 22.
# EDUCATION IN A
# TECH-DRIVEN WORLD

As I start this chapter, my daughter has just been accepted to her dream college in the UK. The process of her schooling (versus mine) has been exciting to follow. I mentioned in the beginning of the book that I was somewhat useless during my first 10 years at school. I am not sure today's generation have the same luxury that is 'to goof off'. There seems to be extremely high expectations set on today's kids, most likely by ambitious parents. I hear horror stories about teenagers studying all evening after school, on top of doing extracurricular activities to boost their CVs. These kids are stressed! Although I can understand (somewhat) why parents push their kids, I disagree with it. My understanding originates from the fact that if you take the top 10% of students from China alone, a country where the kids have been taught to study extremely hard from the age of two or three, those top students outnumber all students in the western world combined, and they're competing for the same place at a university. Personally, we were very lucky. Early on in her schooling, my daughter's teachers asked us not to ask or push her to do homework, not offer to help, and certainly not to force her. They argued that we as parents had done our schooling and now it was our children's turn, and it was their job to motivate their students to do homework and teach the students the consequence of not doing it. God bless Zurich International School; they made my life so much easier! They also taught us something interesting – that they did not know *for what* they were educating our children. That was an odd thing to say but they argued that by the time our children were done with schooling, the world would be a different place without many of the professions we know today. I loved that they stated that so clearly and was impressed, but little did I understand how right it seemed until some years later when I started working with Blockchain. According to World Economic Forums 'The future of jobs' report, it is estimated that for a child just starting school, 65% of the jobs we know today will have disappeared by the time that child graduates from university. It can be assumed that AI, robots, 3D printing, and Blockchain, just to mention a few, will keep developing and boost each other's specialty. The Pew Research Centre states, in their report on the future of jobs and jobs training, that we have already seen technology not only doing the equivalent of some jobs, but in many cases doing it better.[7] Examples are insurance claims adjusters, lawyers, some journalism, financial reporting, hiring managers, psychological testers, etc. In addition, technologies will eliminate the simpler crush jobs of the masses, such as driving trucks, performing middle management and government jobs to name a few. Pew argues that eventually even software programmers will be replaced by technology.

Obviously, these examples alone indicate schooling and job training must be completely re-designed, and with technology, we can look at new ways of enhancing and widening our current education system. From the examples given above, we need an overhaul as it affects low-skilled, middle skilled as well as highly skilled professional groups and raises the following questions for education:

- What roles are needed in a technology driven world?
- What skills, capabilities, and attributes are needed?
- What jobs can be developed or replace another?

I recently attended a small gathering for the 50th birthday of my friend and business partner, Conny. He gave a small speech to the employees of Mountain Partners and a few guests, mainly executives from the corporate world. His message was simple: a business education used to be a great thing but today is worth nothing. Why? It used to be that you would educate yourself for a safe job in a large firm, and for that, you needed a strong business education. He went on to state that those large firms will disappear soon enough, removing that safety net altogether, and that you therefore might as well take a job in a start-up where you can learn on the job and make an impact. Most of the employees in Mountain Partners have business educations but Conny's personal assistant is a lawyer. This led to Conny pointing out that, at least, he could write a contract whereas business people really had not learned anything useful. I agree. You remember Ed (taught me sales in my first job in New York)? What I learned and gained from Ed, they do not and cannot teach you at business school. Based on my experience, they teach you very little ingenuity and out of the box thinking in business school, aside from crafts like finance, accounting, and economics. It was no different at Columbia Business School. Finance, accounting and economics are hard skills and tools you can learn; sales, marketing, strategy etc. cannot be taught by anyone. You need that X factor! You can go through cases and draw your own conclusions, but learning? No. So my recommendation to young people is that they study something where they learn something concrete. Study engineering, medicine, law. And then, if you can, study business on the side. Taking business studies and completing an MBA, as I did, is a waste of time these days. Another thing – no business school can impart leadership skills. They can inspire you (maybe), give you some theory to work with, but great leaders they do not make.

Now, let's dive into the three questions I raised above and start with the roles needed in a tech-driven world.

The World Economic Forum did some research on roles that are currently emerging and those in decline.[8] The up and comers are roles like data analysts and scientists, AI and machine learning specialists, software and application developers, sales and marketing professionals (remember my earlier comment, business *is sales*), big data specialists, digital transformation specialists, new technology (such as Blockchain) specialists, organizational development specialists, and information technologists. It provides a very clear picture - almost all the roles are centered around some specialty in technology. The WEF lists the following roles in decline among the global job landscape: data entry clerks, accountants, book keepers, payroll clerks, administrators, assembly and factory workers, customer service people, auditors, general and operations managers, and postal service clerks. This is happening as you're reading this. Jobs for which hundreds of thousands of young people are currently educating themselves for, are disappearing as we speak. The one take away from this overview is that if you have not found your passion and you are about to enter university, technology seems like a safe bet.

The world has changed drastically over the past century, and unfortunately, education has been left behind; the same courses are on offer decade after decade. Everything has drastically changed over the last 25 years – except the class room setting and education. In Switzerland, a country that ranks high in PISA surveys (surveys of how well school kids perform in academics in different countries), kids are still taught to memorize facts, such as the names of the biggest mountains in Switzerland. It used to make sense when information was scarce, few had access to news etc. But schooling based on absorption through memory is outdated today, there is no value in memorizing these things anymore. Actually, if anything, kids have too much information and they should rather be taught how to make sense of information, how to analyze it, and distinguish between what is important and what is not. And in many places, kids are taught beliefs over facts, and that must also be changed pronto. Schools should focus on what is today called the four Cs: critical thinking, creativity, communication, and collaboration.

A further important step is for schools to include technology from a very early age, with a greater focus on tech in general. Understanding technology will be just as important as being able to read. I argued earlier that if you want to work in the business world, finance and accounting is the language you must learn. Similarly, if you want a job in the future, technology must be something you understand and are comfortable with.

Redesigning the curriculum for a changing job market is a priority, and we are already running behind. Schools in the business of higher education seem to have started eliminating obsolete courses which is a relief. Through technology, education can be easily provided, specialized, and personalized. The old school setting we're familiar with, where desks face a teacher and board will certainly disappear, and lessons will be taught in an online setting. Unfortunately, as education in most countries is government run, we need to place our faith in the private sector to kickstart the re-education of education!

Hopefully, we will see a full roll out of high-quality online courses that can be pieced together from a 'menu' to cater for the education of future specialists and the new roles they will hold. David Karger, a computer science professor at MIT stated, 'Most of what we now call online learning is little more than glorified textbooks, but the future is very promising... Online teaching will increase the reach of the top universities, which will put pressure on lesser universities to demonstrate value. One potential future would be for those universities to abandon the idea that they have faculty teaching their own courses and instead consist entirely of a cadre of teaching assistants who provide support for the students who are taking courses online'. In essence, online teaching from the best to the masses. With technology, the educational sector will boom based on mass availability anywhere, any time. Now that's something to look forward to.

As we change our educational system to provide new skills for future roles, we must also consider the second question raised: what skill sets and attributes do employees need in a highly tech-driven world?

Jack Ma, the founder of Alibaba, is passionate about the radical changes needed to transform education and is advocating skills and attributes young people need that technologies cannot replace. Human soft skills, teamwork, empathy and emotions, arts, creativity, liberal arts (like philosophy), science, and psychology are some great examples of areas requiring re-focus as they are not really emphasized in general schooling today. It's concerning that it takes a Chinese entrepreneur to state this so clearly instead of our elected and paid politicians – whose job it really is.

When I mention skills, I should add that said skills are an aspect of psychology rather than taught competencies, and are human attributes that might not be (directly) taught in school, if at all. Such skills include leadership, design thinking, deliberation, conflict resolution, and innovating to mention a few examples. I believe that some of the most important skills for us to have in life, business or private, are gained through interpersonal experiences and material arts; human bodies in close proximity to other human bodies stimulate real compassion, empathy, vulnerability, and social-emotional intelligence.

PEW research found that skills needed to succeed are curiosity, creativity, taking initiative, multi-disciplinary thinking, and empathy. These are the skills that technology, robots, and machines cannot accomplish, and it will create a change from 'what do you want to be when you grow up?' to 'how do you acquire critical thinking and flexible skills, and an attitude flexible enough to help you in an ever-changing world?' In essence, the education system will need to focus on teaching students to adapt to lifelong learning, constantly developing new skills and capabilities.

The WEF looked into what skills or personal attributes are in growth and decline. Growing skills include analytical thinking and innovation, active learning, creativity and originality, critical thinking and analysis, complex problem solving, leadership, social influence, and emotional intelligence to mention the few topping the list. In decline are endurance, manual dexterity, memory, reading, writing, math, active listening (not sure how these last four got on the list), and visual auditory and speech ability, among others.

To what degree the WEF and PEW have got this right I do not know, but they do paint a picture which supports Jack Ma's idea and certainly places focus on human skills and attributes which computers cannot easily replace, if ever. This shouldn't surprise us here in the business world. Many successful business leaders thrive on personal skills rather than actual competencies. That's why you see them easily switch around from one industry to the other, simply counting on their personal attributes making them successful in whatever they do. Given that we are talking about re-directing the masses to a tech-driven world, we need to find ways said skills can be learned. I am skeptical they can be taught in school and am a firm believer that teaching these in the early development phase is very important for our personal attributes. If I am right, we have to start thinking how to develop functioning, contributing citizens from their day of birth. That sounds scary (almost futuristic) but, on the other hand, it touches on a theme mostly ignored. You need a driver's license to drive a car, an electrical engineering or similar education to be an electrician, a pilot license to fly a plane, a doctor's education plus years of internship to operate on patients, and in Switzerland even a certified course before you can own a dog. However, to have a child, the ability to nurture what could be an immense gift or curse to society, you need no education, license, or permission. Isn't that odd... Is that correct? Is it fair to the new born and fair to society? Looking at society in general, a case can be made that many parents fail, and some fail miserably, but is it the state's job to take the initiative beyond mandatory schooling? This is a very interesting discussion we ought to dive into, and while I won't elaborate on it in this book, I will briefly touch on it in the last chapter. For now, let's just conclude that skills needed for the future job market must be acquired throughout life, from birth to death. The school system must contribute whatever it can by eliminating obsolete teachings that can be googled or aren't necessary in a tech-driven world, and focus on material arts, philosophy, problem solving, creativity, and the rest mentioned above. Can this be done through online courses or does it require human interaction. Most likely the latter, which means schooling in some form will continue. Professor Karger stated that the current college model will remain dominant for quite some time, and that makes sense.

Lastly, the question around new jobs or job categories in a tech-driven world will spring forth.

McKinsey Global Institute made a report in 2017 that focused on answering what scenarios they envision for possible job growth in the future.[9] That is not the same as asking about the creation of new roles, which is almost impossible to predict. As I already mentioned, who predicted app developers 20 years ago? McKinsey came up with six scenarios which eliminated certain jobs and called for the creation of others. They foresee rising incomes and consumption, especially in the emerging markets and they estimate around 250 million new jobs can be created out of the resulting consumerism alone. An aging population with 300 million more people above 65 by 2030 will require health care and personal services, with a potential of 50 to 85 million new jobs by 2030. They highlight development and deployment of technology, where they see a 50% spending increase by 2030. As this mainly requires specialists, the estimate is that it will 'only' create up to 50 million jobs. With a growing population and globalization, investments in infrastructure and building will require jobs and is estimated to create 80 to 200 million new jobs, depending on the investment level. The focus on climate will fuel investments in renewable energy, energy efficiency, and climate adaption, requiring manufacturing, construction, and installation to the tune of 10 million new jobs. And lastly, should the world be smart enough to empower more competent women to work, there will be an increased demand for childcare, early childhood education, cleaning, cooking, and gardening – typically unpaid jobs being done today. This is estimated to create an additional 90 million new jobs. So, this sounds positive and in terms of educational focus, we must be ready to educate more health care providers, engineers, scientists and analysts, technology specialists, and educators, among others. This requires a simple shift in focus and can be done relatively easily.

The broader change in ensuring people are well equipped to deal with this fast-paced world,

from birth to death is a tad more difficult, especially since we don't really know what to expect in terms of job creation and elimination. I do know that we need to attack this issue now, especially since politicians are already discussing a 'citizen's income', a general income for every citizen, independent of them working or not. That should be a last resort, and is typically presented by politicians jumping to conclusions that appeal to a certain demographic. Where are the great leaders who will fearlessly and passionately kickstart the broader changes to the education sector, or should education be left to the private sector as they usually manage dynamic situations better? And if so, should that change not be driven by a political leader who would ensure we achieve consensus on this?

Education is an important tool and solution to many of the world's pressing issues, such as income equality, gender equality, equal opportunity, social changes, technological challenges, and economic problems. At the same time, education has had little to no innovation and the idea of educating oneself from 'birth to death' has been ignored for the most part. We need great leaders to step up and become the catalyst for this much needed educational change!

# 23.
# WHAT ARE
# COMPANIES FOR?

When I worked for Fidelity Investments, it was the largest asset manager in the world and accounted for roughly 10% of the daily trading volume on the New York Stock Exchange. It was a huge investor, influencing companies and their stock prices. Fidelity's mantra was return, return, return, and it was logical: if investors don't get a return, they won't invest and since many companies compete for investors, they are totally focused on maximizing profitability and returns. I remember having many 'stimulating' discussions with my wife, who profoundly challenged the mantra's simplicity. I heard her arguments for social responsibility but could not relate to it in my job at that time. That was 20 years ago, and today I fully admit she had some great reflections. When you do your homework and realize the extent companies go through to maximize profit and returns, it's not difficult to understand that it's not an optimal situation. With problems such as extreme unhealthy food, dangerous products, tremendous pollution, child labor, and exploitation of countries, it's way past time to admit companies need to be held accountable in their focused pursuit of profit. Inequality is slap bang in the middle of it through low labor cost and high profit to the company shareholders (just to give you the most obvious example). When I started writing this chapter, my favorite paper, *The Economist*, had a whopper of a cover title: 'WHAT ARE COMPANIES FOR?' I have been reading the Economist since

1988 and cannot remember this question being asked – ever! Social/ corporate responsibility often cropped up, especially as it has been a hot issue in the last decade, and every company had designed some sort of pro forma 'social responsibility' (a.k.a. lip service project) to add in their yearly shareholder report. But maybe it's a sign that we are at the tipping point. The reason *The Economist* took this particular question up was because in the week, 180 of America's biggest bosses pledged their firms' purpose was no longer to serve shareholders alone but also customers, staff, suppliers, and communities. Although this was said with (probably) good intentions, it also raised more than a few questions. Have they really *not* considered customers and employees before? Sure, they have, but **only** to maximize profits. Or, could this just be a pre-emptive measure to avoid further regulation...

At the time of penning this chapter, Trump is still President so legislation and restrictions does not seem like a short-term threat. Then again, Democrats might win the next election and things might change. However, I believe the real driving force is the big bosses realizing that we might have reached the peak of capitalism and something needs to be done...

Capitalism has served the world well (to an extent), but there seems to be a general belief that capitalism alone might not best serve the world going forward. Capitalism in terms of shareholder value started in the US in the 1970s, replacing a managed capitalism in which companies, governments, and unions 'managed' the economy. It really took off in 1990 after Harvard Business Review published an article introducing the idea that CEOs should be paid in stocks, to align them with their owners' company values. This gave birth to the phrase 'maximize shareholder value' and it's had a good run for many years. There are now clear signs that the younger generation in particular is challenging this. They are looking for purpose, for something to believe in, and to be part of something greater than a high paying job that destroys the world in some way. That is wonderful news – I see it in my daughter and her friends. They are certainly more engaged in world issues than I was at that age. My daughter completed a Social Enterprise course at Stanford when she was 16 years old (I will spare you how I spent my summer at the same age!), so there is a definite shift. During a long drive with her this summer from Vienna (she worked in a tech start-up as an intern) to Budapest, she explained the issues surrounding Monsanto, the biotech company, stating she would never work there and would prefer to boycott their products. Judging by the news coverage, she is certainly not alone and children and youngsters now have platforms to share their views, so Monsanto, look out!

Her generation, at least some of the ones I meet, also seem very aware of the use and abuse of child labor, animal exploitation, as well as mass polluting firms. We shouldn't rely alone on the younger generations, although they seem savvier regarding differentiating between right and wrong! Where is my generation's ethics and where are our politicians? It's no secret that politicians have been ineffective in dealing with these issues as they are often gridlocked and, not forgetting the heart of the matter, influenced by lobbyists and paid off by 'political donors' i.e. large corporations. The impact of shareholder value on inequality has been clearly illustrated by the fact that workers' shares of the value firms create have declined in the flourishing age of capitalism. In addition, only 50% of American households (and that is very high compared to other countries) have exposure to the stock market, and this 50% is heavily curved in favor of the wealthy elite. Nevertheless, capitalism brought growth and jobs and will continue to do so, which means we cannot get rid of it entirely. So where does that leave us? How should we look at this? What should potential leaders do? How do we make sure that corporations serve both their owners as well as the broader society at large?

It is very rare that I disagree with analysis and conclusions presented in The Economist, likely because they are based on research and facts, even if they're presented by an opinionated journalist. It's hard to disagree with facts (unless you're a Trumper) but when it comes to the more opinionated arguments, one needs to be alert. In this case, The Economist argues that the well-meaning, more socially responsible form of capitalism will do more harm than good. Their arguments were based on two things: lack of accountability and lack of dynamism. They argued that many industries are dominated by few firms and that leaves but a few leaders to decide what is good for society, which of course would be wrong (although it might always have been so). As for dynamism, they argued that to thrive through change, firms have to forsake some stakeholders. Really? Surely there must be further reflections and better perspectives?!

Elisabeth Warren, a 2020 US presidential candidate, suggested that businesses receive an operating license. If they misbehave that license can be revoked, similarly to how restaurants are monitored: find a rat, we close you down. She hopes this would push firms to pursue broader social goals. I personally worry about the execution of this idea, but it's certainly interesting. Personally, I'm not in favor of allowing politicians to 'control' businesses to that extent. Although politicians can, and most likely should, consider incentives for businesses to serve a broader purpose; political solutions should be a last resort.

Let's go back to the roots of capitalism, the economic system based on private ownership and free markets regulating itself to the best standard – in theory anyway. The belief is that if a company is solely focused on making profit, they will harm other stakeholders and somehow be punished or pushed aside by competitors, or their stock will be dumped by the owners. That doesn't reflect reality. Shareholders want returns and if it's there, they don't seem to bother asking questions. They are, however, being punished by the short-term focus listed companies are having today. Running a company for long-term growth and profit is a completely different thing than maximizing quarterly results. In essence, with a focus on quarterly results, CEOs are extracting value for shareholders rather than creating value for shareholders. Just look at all the share buyback programs taking place as one example. Instead of spending money on innovation and acquiring new customers, companies simply buy their own stock to increase returns. This used to be viewed as stock market manipulation and was illegal in the US until Republicans legalized it in 1982. Jack Ma, the Founder of Alibaba, has stated that customers are number one, employees are number two, and shareholders come in at number three. And he's not alone in this outlook. More voices are starting to question the 'maximizing shareholder value' doctrine, especially if you add short-term focus, where it becomes a value destruction strategy. You cut costs and spare innovations to maximize profit now, but this comes at the cost of future profit – bad for the economy, bad for jobs, and, in the end, bad for the shareholders (unless they are simply traders). CEOs are facing a downward spiraling dilemma which provides an opportunity for change, but does free market capitalism fuel this change, as it's supposed to? I'm not sure what the clear answer is but there is very little shareholder activism. Most shares are held by the company's management and institutional investors. Management do whatever they want, such as awarding themselves large bonuses for having solved a huge screw up by paying a huge fine (making the owners pay for management's mistake, to be clear). Institutional investors do not organize themselves and try to force management to act sensibly, instead they end up selling the stock. To what degree is it right or wrong for institutional investors to be active investors? It's an interesting question with many good arguments for and against but the simple fact remains that most companies are run unchecked by their shareholders, and that is never a good thing as it results in crazy, chaotic management behavior.

When I was drafting this chapter, Boeing was facing claims it sold its 737 MAX planes with dangerous software. Boeing states it's taking action to ensure the safety of the 737. Goldman Sachs is faced with criminal charges in the famous Malaysian 1MDB scandal, the biggest corruption scandal ever. Goldman states it's working with the investigators. Monsanto just faced a verdict that it failed to warn customers their weed killer product could cause cancer. The company says it will appeal but they seem to be on the losing end of the stick in this battle. Wells Fargo has admitted to creating three and half million unauthorized bank accounts. They state they are working to rebuild trust with their stakeholders. Facebook's data practice scandals are under investigation in several countries. They say there is a need for a more active role for governments and regulators. Equifax had the personal data of 146 million customers stolen and is being sued for negligence. They state protecting data is their highest priority.

All the above are examples of crazy, irrational, largely uncontrolled behavior. In a free market setting how can these companies survive? Well, first and foremost, many of these companies are oligopolies and they get away with a lot. Lack of competition is a major issue, meaning if we want to eliminate bad actors then entry barriers should be lowered. That might be something politicians could help with, more so because it is something fully embraced by the capitalist model. We need basic instruments to ensure every industry and company competes fairly. Doing so will provide consumers with better and broader choices, and that can make a positive impact. We can buy a good or service from a company that best fits our values. If we are worried about pollution, we buy earth friendly goods or services from an eco-friendly firm. If we are worried about poisonous products, we buy natural, do no harm products. If we do not accept child labor, we buy from transparent and ethical companies. If people were provided with better information, transparency, understanding, and choice company bosses would have to step up and put the consumer first, and that would dictate what suppliers they use and how to compensate and deal with their employees. Peter Drucker stated back in 1954 that 'there is only one valid purpose of a corporation: to create a customer.' Making money is the result, not the goal.

Increased competition can also bring an increase in accountability. It forces companies to anticipate and reflect on the changing preferences of customers, workers and regulators. The digital economy promised increased competition and a democratization of businesses. Everybody, it was assumed, could simply start an online business and compete with the 'established' players, and that held true in the beginning. Today though, as stated earlier, a few digital businesses dominate. Since 1990, we have seen an increase in the consolidation and concentration of businesses in America, rather than a democratization.

The free markets have not worked as hoped, nor did digitalization. Political leaders must ensure healthy regulation and enforce antitrust rules to a higher degree, with the intent of eliminating lobbying and cronyism. Politicians shouldn't manage the business world and the markets but simply ensure healthy competition is possible at all levels, as well as guaranteeing full transparency. You might have heard of the tough Dane, Margrethe Vestager, often referred to as 'the rich world's most powerful trustbuster' who boldly takes on one dominating tech company after the other. We need more individuals like her who, hand in hand with great political leadership, can foster competition on all levels.

It is worth noting that most of the 180 'big boss' signatories mentioned earlier are working for oligopolies, who can over-charge customers and who worry about lowering entry barriers for new competitors. It seems ensuring fair play and a competitive spirit is up to politicians as we cannot trust company bosses with that task.

To sum up, strong business leaders must manage firms with a broader purpose in mind than to simply maximize shareholder value. To ensure that, great political leaders must rally and focus on measures that ensure transparency of business conduct and include measures that foster competition at all levels. This is a much better role for politicians than regulating or 'managing' businesses. Political leaders can create the right framework and with that the consumers (us) will be able to 'manage' businesses via choosing what we buy and from whom. This also solves the issue raised by *The Economist* as it is not up to (oligopolies) managers to decide what social responsibility their firm should focus on, if any. It will be the broader masses and that's exactly how it should be!

# 24.
# WEALTH DISTRIBUTION
# POLICIES

Normally, it a waste of time to discuss any potentially great solution that ultimately relies on the doings of politicians (as can be seen from the last two chapters, we are still waiting for great political leaders in these important fields). I do believe that many politicians start out with a decent cause, a strong belief, or a passion to improve the world. Unfortunately, to survive in the political jungle, and that seems to be their main objective after a short time, they make compromises on their beliefs and philosophies, simply to remain in power. To remain in power, they are willing to, say, agree and vote for what keeps them in power, not what they believe in. Politicians are sub-optimized and therefore get very little done. In this book, I haven't put my hopes in politicians, but leaders. True visionaries that forego their ego to follow their beliefs and principles. On that note, let's look into what potentially strong and decent political leaders can do to solve inequality.

There are several options to address inequality. Obviously, redistribution of wealth is the obvious one, and achieved mainly through income taxes. There is stopping corruption dead in its tracks as well as closing loop holes for tax avoidance. Doing away with trade barriers all together, and allowing underdeveloped countries a chance to produce and export to wealthy countries can also be solutions. Also, charity and foreign aid, which have been used for a long time, the latter often with questionable results. I include the total free movement of people and workers, allowing the poor to join wealthy economies, and while this is already in progress it's not on a grand scale and definitely not 100% through desired or legal immigration. And finally, simply raising taxes on wealth or inheritance. All these, and other initiatives, could play a major role in addressing inequality. Now, which ones are the most effective?

When reading the following, you might want to keep two things in mind. First, I grew up in Denmark where my dad paid up to 80% in income tax. My family was not rich by today's standards but certainly upper-middle class. We had a nice house, two cars, and a motor boat. You pay a 180% luxury tax as well as 25% sales tax on cars so a VW Golf that might cost €30,000 in Germany would cost close to €100,000 in Denmark. You pay that price for your car after having paid (today) 65% income tax on everything above €70,000. To buy a VW Golf with cash in Denmark, you must make roughly €200,000, in Germany you need around €55,000. If you visit Copenhagen today, after knowing this, you will be amazed by the multitude of beautiful cars driving through the streets, and the many restaurants that are full capacity seven days a week. On the other hand, education and health care are free. Every Dane has full access to quality healthcare as well as good schooling. You're also paid a salary to study in university. This is called the Scandinavian model, and I won't judge it as there's enough global debate about the Scandinavian model already. Secondly, I live in Switzerland now and not only that, but the lowest taxed region (Kanton). I pay around 18% income tax but if I move one kilometer closer to Zurich (which I have no intention of doing), my income tax would more than double. Switzerland has tax competition and the local tax authorities treats you like a customer because they know you can choose where to live and pay taxes (no surprise, Porsche is a normal car in my neighborhood). Looking at both countries, Switzerland and Denmark are two extremes, at least when it comes to taxation. Again, I am not judging this, but thought it fair that I disclose my choice. I would like to mention one other thing since I alluded to it earlier in the book. In Denmark you are brought up with strong values: that things should be fair and nobody is better than anybody else. Switzerland, on the other hand, is the most money-oriented country I have ever seen, and I have visited almost 100 countries in my life. People are extremely focused on money and status; keep in mind, Switzerland was partly built by money secreted away for crooks and criminals, almost none of whom have been prosecuted or gone to jail. Try that in Denmark: one little tax mistake and you go to jail for a very long time.

Let's head back to the earlier choices I mentioned for closer consideration. To do so, we will have to do it at a higher level and more generically, as it would differ from country to country and region to region.

In general, I am against simply raising income taxes to have more for distribution purposes. People need an incentive to work and extremely high taxes have generally not proven popular in the long-term. Think about this: if you pay most of your income in tax and see it redistributed to people who might work significantly less than you, or not at all, that feeling of resentment really starts to build on a grander scale and can divide a country. Most studies support that simply raising income taxes is not good for the economy, the population, and even the poor, who depend on finding others who can afford to give them a job. Our economy relies on people being incentivized to work, create value, and take risks as entrepreneurs. Add to this scenario that most governments are lousy at administrating how funds are collected and used. But it's interesting to know that if you query whether income taxes should be raised, the Swiss population will say no, including some of the 'poor' (40% of Swiss households have difficulties making ends meet). By contrast, the Danish population would be open to it, including some in the wealthier tier. This alludes to it not being merely an economical phenomenon but a cultural one as well.

As a Dane, things must play out fairly. That means I am more interested in people actually paying taxes owed, rather than raising income tax, which will simply result in more people becoming embroiled in big scheme tax avoidance. Keep in mind, most (honest) wealthy people can chose to live where they want, but if they live in a certain country and earn an income or have their company registered there then they should pay full taxes as owed to that particular country.

Collecting extra trillions by getting rid of corruption allows the public purse to fund the public with social welfare programs that reduces and eliminates systemic inequality. The South African Revenue Agency has 40 people (only!) working to curb tax avoidance from large corporations. A single large corporation has 40 + lawyers and accountants on their books, designed to ensure they can shift profit in a technically 'legal' way. Curbing illicit flows is a holistic solution to predatory inequality that is a deliberate product of the system, not a symptom of a natural incapacity to progress. An artificially poor or bankrupt state has no money to invest in its own economic and political development. In essence, inequality would be partly eliminated by the simple fact that people and corporations would pay the taxes they are obliged to, and those funds would be available to support the poorer demographic. It is estimated that the lost tax revenue by companies shifting profit every year is around $600 billion alone! And that is just from shifting profit! We're not even counting direct tax avoidance, which is higher for private individuals than corporations. It is estimated that around $30 trillion worth of private wealth is held off shore, mainly to avoid taxation.

Politicians must do everything in their power to close any loophole, whether it is within a country's tax code or law, through tax havens, or tax avoidance schemes by lawyers, banks, advisors etc. Can this be achieved realistically? Denmark has proved it. Danish politicians have worked hard on eliminating every single tax avoidance opportunity and made it a highly punishable offence. 'How serious'? You can get the same jail time for tax avoidance as you do for murder. Now, feel free to wiggle out of that. When I had my bank in Switzerland, I had Danes contacting me with money abroad i.e. not declared in Denmark. When I had helped them understand their real legal situation, they were willing to give the money away simply to remove the risk of going to jail. They initially thought they could hide it somewhere else, then they wanted to give it all to charity, take it out in cash, or eventually even give it to me, but none of these were viable options. No matter what they did, they had already broken the law and would have to live in fear of being discovered. Their banks knew the problem they faced and therefore asked them to take their money out, but there was nowhere to go; the Danish tax system is both strong and pure, with a culture that supports this whereas most other countries do not have this. What countries essentially need are strong good leaders that take the tax avoidance case forward without caving in to lobbyist influences or being mocked by the entitled. Bernie Sanders, a US presidential candidate is an ideal representation of the above, although not my favorite candidate. Let's hope we get to hear more of these voices in other countries. Remember, my point is about collecting the income taxes, not raising them. The more income taxes are raised, the more people will try to cheat making the move counterproductive. Trump stated in his campaign that he paid little taxes because he is 'smart'. Well, we need to eliminate these loopholes allowing people to be 'smart' as it undermines our entire society and the world at large. Something Trump obviously does not care about...

Next is corruption. Corruption in its simplest form is people using a position of power to extort money from someone else. This is no different than stealing. There is nothing positive about corruption and nothing good about the people doing it or benefiting from it. Many corrupt individuals have become extremely wealthy. I have personally witnessed this in Switzerland where Eastern European government employees, with extremely low salaries, are looking to buy tremendously expensive ski apartments. There are no doubts how they end up affording that. Corruption is unfortunately embedded in most countries and, in some countries, it is a standard practice and assumed to be normal.

Corruption is viewed through a misdiagnosed lens. We fixate on 'public officials abusing public office for private gain' yet research shows more than 60% of illicit flows from Africa is tax avoidance by large corporations. Sixty per cent might raise eyebrows and appear shocking but if you research this field in-depth, you find corporations provide kickbacks in the forms of tens of millions to corrupt politicians in order to facilitate the kind of illicit flows (money flowing against the purpose of the law) that is impoverishing the continent. Rather than quoting statistics and endless examples, let me pick one example as reported by the Global Anti-Corruption Consortium, a partnership between CCRP and Transparency International on www.occrp.org, recognized as a very reliable source. 10 For illustrative purposes, I will simply summarize what their research concluded in 2018 about a well reported case but will not use real names, instead I'll refer to company A, company B etc.

*The story starts in 2006, where a Scandinavian billionaire, in his role as CEO of company A (a giant crude oil trading firm founded by him and an ally of President Putin), was concerned that the US might cut the company's main source of oil and therefore started searching for new sources of crude oil.*

*Company A identified the Republic of Congo's Moho-Bilondo oilfield. They contacted a special adviser to the Congolese President who then paved the way for a lucrative deal for company A, resulting in about US$ 2.2 billion from 22 tankers of crude oil it was able to purchase from Congo in 2010 to 2012. In 2011, more than 20 percent of the company's global profits of $327.9 million came straight from that impoverished tropical country. The operation violated Congolese law as the shipments were purchased without the required public tender and because of payments made to government officials, which were derived from the oil revenues and the inflated loan fees that company A charged the Congolese state oil company, according to an analysis by Public Eye,* *an anti-corruption organization.*

*Behind a veil of shell companies and offshore accounts, company A facilitated payments through company B, of $48 million, after which company A won favorable trade deals in another three African countries. The funds were transferred between Switzerland and Hong Kong as well as through Mauritius, Luxembourg, and Monaco. To disguise the true relationship between company A and company B, they were listed as shipping fees.*

*The Ivory Coast was one of the countries and, in 2008, a contract for what looked like a one-year agreement was signed between company A and company B. Through B, company A sent payments of $7.6 million to officials close to the President between 2010 and 2011. Through Swiss and Belgian banks, including BSI Ltd and BNP Fortis, five payments were intended for three other state officials: The President's uncle who headed the country's refinery, a presidential economic advisor and the head of the country's petroleum company. Because of the political crisis which later developed in the country, it is not clear if the payments ever reached their intended recipients. The records indicate that after the payments were made, company A was given access to more than 3.1 million barrels of the nation's oil in preferential deals. Company A also provided for pre-payment of about $90 million worth of oil to the Ivorian regime. As would occur later in Congo, the money to pay officials was skimmed off the top of the oil shipments. For example, company B received from company A $2 per barrel as a "profit sharing" fee that the contract says was for its help in negotiating for and exporting Ivorian oil.*

*In this case, company B received money though the company had played no role in the extraction or transportation of the oil. Part of these funds were promptly routed to offshore bank accounts. Company B transferred funds to another company, which then immediately paid out significant sums – some 70 percent of which were intended for public officials. Meanwhile, company A raked in the profits – and looked elsewhere in Africa to build on its success.*

*A shell company which appeared to be used only for funneling payments was rewarded with a service fee of two to three percent. This pattern was repeated a number of times. Company B made a large number of payments through its maze of offshore companies, apparently on behalf of company A. In return, company A received highly profitable contracts.*

*Through company B, payments were then sent to the Congolese President, his wife, his son, and his nephew, among other Congolese insiders including a powerful presidential advisor. The President told media, "Congo is a sovereign state that has the legal standing to choose who it does business with, as all countries do, all of which is done in a thoroughly transparent and legal manner." A key facilitator in the scheme, frequently asked company B's founder for money to buy luxury cars, rent property, and give his children allowances, according to emails seen by OCCRP and Médor. The family received these payments through shell companies. For its pains, company A made double the going rate per barrel in profit. Company B's patronage ate through Congo's oil revenues. About 20 percent of profits from the 22 shipments company A sold — amounting to around $22 million — went to the benefit of the Congo's ruling family and key officials, documents show.*

*Eventually, authorities came to suspect company A was laundering money and bribing government officials overseas. Swiss prosecutors were suspicious of accounts held at Clariden Leu, a Zurich bank, that conducted more than $22 million of transactions in just a few months. In January 2012, police raided company A's Africa desk, seized internal communications, and launched criminal proceedings. In 2018, a former company A oil trader pleaded guilty in a Swiss court to bribing public officials to secure oil cargoes from the Republic of Congo and Ivory Coast. Company A stated that they "wholly reject the possibility of a conscious and desired involvement of any other employee or executive."*

*On October 19, 2019, Swiss federal prosecutors ordered company A to pay US$ 95 million after finding it guilty of corruption in Ivory Coast and Congo.*

*This is one story out of many endless examples reported and it better illustrates the issues than countless statistics. Another more famous example centered around 1 Malaysia Berhad (1MDB) where at least $3.5 billion disappeared from Malaysia's state-owned fund in just five years. Seventeen current and former Goldman Sachs banking executives are now in court on criminal charges.*

*Funds were channeled through shell companies around the world, including the US, Luxembourg, Malaysia, Singapore, UAE, and of course, Switzerland. The most senior accused is the Chairman of Goldman Sachs, Asia and he has already pleaded guilty to some of the charges. The bank itself, as is 'standard practice' in these cases, calls him a rough wild employee. Denmark, a country that rates as one of the least corruptible in the world, had their largest bank, Danske Bank, involved in large-scale money laundering through their branch in the Baltics.*

The above goes to show that corruption has become part and parcel in standard business operating procedures, and the largest corruption issues point to the channeling of illegal funds around the world through dummy shell companies, eventually ending up in the wrong hands. It fuels inequality and injustice, to the ruination of the most vulnerable. How do we tackle something that has operated in opaque muddy waters, largely unchecked for so long?

Solving the problem needs a multi-pronged attack – at the same time:

a)  Legislative measures targeting sources of corrupt activities ranging from beneficial ownership law to disclosure of all upstream and downstream mineral contracts, tender processes, appointment of board members to state owned entities etc.

b)  Systemic legislation, strengthening democratic rule of law such as Anti-Corruption Acts, Protected Disclosures Acts, Witness Protection Acts

c)  Autonomous bodies such as Press Ombudsman, Public Protector etc.

d) Strong and free media, and other resources to hold power to account

e) Cross-border automatic information exchange, country-by-country reporting.

As long as legal and financial secrecy jurisdictions and virtual self-regulation of intra-company corporate activity exist in the business landscape without automatic information exchange, country-by-country reporting, and beneficial ownership, capital can 'rent' sovereignty of other countries to pass-thru capital. The quickest solution is taxing illicit financial flows to secrecy jurisdictions. This would penalize the benefit and disincentivize the act itself.

Blockchain can provide a solution, but we still require great leaders to step up and ensure the justice process will be impartial, and this is no small feat. A great leader that stands up, clearly articulating the problem as well as the solution, will likely accumulate many enemies, usually the most powerful people in said country. In many places, it is a difficult and dangerous fight, but history has shown that strong leaders have existed and will do whatever it takes to see justice done. When they do, it will have tremendous impact on a country's improved wealth equality, opportunity, and economic growth, ultimately benefiting the masses.

Now let's briefly look at globalization, meaning world-wide trade which has made the world richer, but not benefited all equally. Developed countries have protected themselves all the way, for example when providing 'foreign aid', the aid was typically tied to purchasing machinery from the donor country, often not really helping. Also look at the EU's farming subsidies. Around 40% of the EU budget goes to farmers in the EU. Those funds could do a lot of good in the developing world, and instead of eating shitty, outrageously expensive locally-grown tomatoes, we could partake in delicious, natural, sun-ripened tomatoes from Africa. Basic economic sensibility says a product should be produced where it can be produced the best and cheapest. Trade barriers, trade tariffs, and import regulations work against that fundamental principle. The potential for true free trade is enormous but, of course, unpopular with the developed world's populist politicians. It will take a strong leader to stand up and explain in clear terms the opportunities such trade can bring about in terms of wealth creation and better income distribution on a global scale.

A more dramatic step than free movement of goods would be the free movement of people. We have seen clear trends in urban migration, particularly when job opportunities are involved. However, things are tougher (border control) if we're looking at immigration policies, especially in these times. In the 60s, Germany invited cheap labor, mainly from Turkey, to help build their country and businesses. One of the key reasons the US has such an enduring economy is that they've always accepted cheap foreign labor. Europe is aging, and younger, cheaper workers are needed, as well as highly skilled people. Unfortunately, due to the influence of biased media and the stupidity of politicians, immigration has been mishandled and become an extremely sensitive issue – we are a long way from free movement of people around the world but it's something we should discuss to ensure we can successfully integrate a new workforce and community. But with the right measures, such as easing trade barriers, eliminating corruption, and the collection of taxes, fewer people would move (why would they if they can live and work productively in their own countries?). A combination of the right measures would relativize immigration. As we are currently going the other way, where Trump's vision of a 'beautiful wall' is the most dramatic example, hoping for the free movement of people (to solve inequality) likely won't happen any time soon.

There are many other politically-possible solutions, such as greater efforts to educate women, setting (higher) minimum salaries, reducing juvenile crime to mention a few. With so many options available, politicians have no excuse to sit by and watch the world go by!

I praised Bill Gates' 'Giving pledge' earlier and politicians could take that a step further: set a high, say 50%, inheritance tax on any bigger fortune (to be defined). Individuals can still collect whatever they want in life but it would stop the following generations being simply born ultra-wealthy without having the know how or responsibility to handle such a gift. When the top 1% have a 50%, inheritance tax, it might have a bigger redistribution effect that anything else. Build your firm, buy your cars, houses, art, and yachts, but your offspring will have to partly make their own living. Instead of giving the millions or billions you earned to one or two people, let it benefit the population that needs it, the people that allowed you to collect it in the first place. You could argue that the people inheriting the money invest in companies that create jobs etc., but those companies might hire cheap labor and achieve greater domination, as has often been the case. The legacy you leave behind with a substantial inheritance tax, would be better for the economy and the population. Who knows, some of the otherwise struggling people now receiving education, health care, and other support would maybe go and build their own business. They would create jobs and pay taxes, rather than just receiving a bare minimum salary while the people inheriting the money take out 'tax optimization' investments for themselves alone. Of course, politicians would need to address the practicality of this as this type of wealth is usually tied to one company where liquidation is not an easy or desired solution. In Denmark, the solution is to put wealth in foundations with yearly distribution to good causes (I financed my MBA with grants from such foundations). It limits family dynasties and spreads wealth more equally. It would not stop wealth creation as people are greedy and want to build extravagant fortunes, despite a high inheritance tax; such is human nature. I believe that during this period of the highest wealth inequality in history, with mostly tax-free inheritance and slow increases in general incomes, we are faced with a spiraling inequality effect, unless something drastic is implemented, such as a high inheritance tax.

Is there any scientific support for my proposed drastic measure?

I looked and yes, indeed there is! Thomas Piketty in his book Capital in the Twenty-First Century gives rock solid arguments for why my broader idea of taxing capital, in one form or the other, might be the best idea to truly solve inequality. His book is 800-pages long, a masterpiece complete with research and analysis which humbles my effort to even write about it, let alone try to summarize. In short, his book analyzes income and capital/wealth inequality and his conclusion is that a progressive, yearly capital tax is needed to best solve inequality. As I mentioned earlier, we have seen a drastic rise in super manager salaries versus the average employee, something he also points out. That has a big effect on income inequality, but a more important factor highlighted in Piketty's book is the problem of wealth distribution.

Wealth distribution used to be extremely uneven, especially up to the First World War. With the two World Wars and their devastating effects, the capital to income ratio declined, meaning a fairer distribution emerged (unfortunately, for the wrong reason). Today, the ratio has (again) reached those ultimate heights seen before the Wars. One contributing factor has been that of booming stock and real estate prices, and other asset appreciations, making the return on capital higher than the growth of the economy. This has resulted in a steady increase in wealth concentration and a very high level of capital to income ratio. With no foreseen shift in economic growth rates, particular in the developed world where most of the wealth is held, inheritance of these fortunes automatically becomes an explorative issue if we want better distribution of wealth going forward. This point is dramatized in Piketty's book where he takes France, as an example, and proves that nearly all capital stock in a given year is accumulated from inheritance. It should be noted that inheritance, in the broader definition, includes gifts to children and other dependents while the holder is still alive. The majority of gifts are typically given an average of 10 years before death and are typically real estate. Nevertheless, it is a transfer of wealth, like inheritance, and nothing else so it must be accounted as such. Unless anything changes, fortunes will be passed from one generation to the next, increasing faster than the general income level of the masses, and we will be faced with an ever-increasing concentration of wealth controlled by an extremely small minority, thus increasing inequality. This is something society and humankind need to address urgently, and though it raises the question of government efficiency, there shouldn't be an argument around 'should we or should we not'. I point out that the intention should not be for redistribution to the less fortunate directly as that is a very questionable and unsuccessful political act. Instead, governments could better focus on what they are supposed to do: provide education and free healthcare for all, and perhaps a pension for people who were not fortunate enough to save enough for old age. By doing so, we would tackle equal opportunity rather than redistribution, where children of the less fortunate could receive excellent education and healthcare on par with the wealthier group, thereby positively contributing to the economy. That is a redistribution of social rights. I mentioned something called the Scandinavian model earlier; well, my drastic proposal is going in that direction and, let me remind you, Scandinavian countries are always rated among the top five happiest and best places to live in the world. Definitely something worth considering!

As a last remark to my proposal of a very high inheritance tax, let me highlight that Piketty argues a yearly capital tax of around 1–2%. I argue an inheritance tax of 50%. If your wealth is in, say, a company you own, paying a yearly wealth tax might be difficult and could disrupt the business. Given that you are a great value generator, for yourself, the economy, and society, we should avoid that. Let entrepreneurs and value creators flourish, let them create what they can and be motivated by enjoying the fruits of their work as long as they live.

So, to solve inequality, I believe the initial focus of great business and political leaders must be to eradicate corruption, maybe with the help of Blockchain technology, hand-in-hand with stopping tax avoidance (also maybe with the help of Blockchain), and certainly global coordination against tax heavens, as well as taxing inheritance at 50%.

I might be right; I might be wrong. Piketty might be right or wrong, but let's start having the right discussions because something needs to be done, and that 'something' will require some drastic measures. Great leaders of the world, you need to step up! If we continue this way, civil war may soon become a reality. Remember this: the last major disruption to the high levels of inequality were two World Wars. As intelligent human beings, that should make us think...

# PART IV

## YOU

# 25.
# IT'S TIME TO STEP UP

I considered letting the book end here but read a headline in a Swiss newspaper that really hit me. The article focused on Swiss banks 'aiding' Venezuelan politicians to steal money from what is now one of the poorest countries in the world. Billions of dollars are plundered by corrupt, greedy self-serving politicians – at the same time the population starves and the country defaults on its debt. Venezuela is close to my heart as I have been there several times and made many good friends there. Most have left by now; a choice they're lucky to have as they are the privileged few with money and connections enabling them to get to their houses or apartments in Miami. I was on the phone two days ago with my good, very well-to-do friend Antonio, who confided in me that he was considering leaving at this point. Apparently, everything had become as expensive as Switzerland without the safety and functionality of Switzerland. I mentioned in an earlier chapter that Venezuela has the largest oil reserves in the world and was one of the ten richest countries in the world in the 60s, but corrupt leaders have now totally ruined the country. This isn't unusual, we have seen this happen in countries all over the world – the major issue is that Swiss banks are facilitating this fraud, embezzlement, and money laundering. The irony is that the President of Switzerland met Trump and agreed to give financial support to Venezuela just two weeks before this article appeared. Naturally, these are double (moral) standards at the highest level, which is nothing unusual for

Switzerland. Then again, Swiss banks have been called out for money laundering, especially in the last ten years and major improvements have been 'forced' on them. But that raises the question: how can this be happening today? Are Swiss bank managers so greedy, so corrupt that nothing else matters? The answer in my opinion: YES! I have hope (perhaps this is naive) that people in powerful positions, like those on the board of Swiss banks, Swiss politicians, and politicians of Venezuela, will step up to be great leaders. But, based on the actions we witness, I wonder if there are enough leaders standing up for the right things. I look around and see few. I scan the news and find almost none. So, what do we do? How do we make the world better, if great leaders do not step up?

Since I started writing this book, it often comes up in dinner conversations and the like. When I meet new people, I enjoy mentioning that I'm a writer. Although that is a gross overstatement, it leads to fascinating conversations – all interesting and extremely helpful to me. I've noticed that I tend to seek out conversations with people who are very aware and reflective of their lives and the world we live in. These conversations allow me to listen and learn, and I'm forced to reflect and question my own opinions and beliefs. Some of these people happen to be very spiritual, and I observed that there are few to none of my 'usual' circle seated at the table (the bankers, lawyers, investment managers etc.) that have so defined my circle of friends for most of my life.

I've had thousands of dinners where we discussed stock markets, house prices, favorite hotels, and cars, but these conversations occurred among people who saw things the same way, more or less shared the same opinions, or when not in agreement, they tried to convince each other 'I'm right, you're wrong'. This changes drastically when there are more reflective and spiritually inclined people at the table. You pick up that they speak very little, listen very carefully, and only offer their reflections once asked. They don't try to convince anyone of anything but rather try to understand why someone has a certain belief or conviction. This makes for a very different conversation, a much more interesting conversation. Rather than a dinner party divided between liking Trump or hating him, it suddenly becomes a reflective conversation around his policies, and whether they work or not. Or perhaps trying to understand why a person who seems intelligent and decent supports Trump. I have learned a great deal from such conversations and started enjoying them so much that 'classic' conversations have started to bore me; I now avoid dinners with people where the conversation is predictable.

Why do I bring this up? The Venezuelan story: a common issue everywhere and I fear that it's not enough to hope or wait on a few great leaders to change the world. In addition, based on the people I've met the last years, I now believe there are people out there with alternative or supplementary solutions to solving wealth inequality, as well as many other issues the world is faced with. To carry you on my train of thought of what I have learned from people that have inspired me over the last few years, I first need to share my broader view of what I feel is wrong with the human race today. To do this, allow me to summarize and expound some of the opinions I've already shared.

This book positively acknowledges that the world is doing better than ever and that new technologies actually stand to make it even better, if applied correctly. But at the same time, we have somehow come to a point where we, the human race, elect Trump as the leader of the free world. Please forget Trump, he is just one out of many narcissistic demagogues in this world but we have to ask how 64 million people arrived at the decision that voting for him was the best thing. Obama made a great speech about this issue in which he kept repeating, 'How did we get there, how could this happen?' We have the world doing great, a long period of peace, people around the world working and trading with each other creating wealth in many poor countries. Global citizens are more willing to help others, independent of where these individuals live. However, it's not only the US placing a divider in the office. We see a movement to extremism in many parts of the world, including first world countries. Trump and other populist leaders cannot spoil the world alone – they need us, the human race, the voters, individual citizens to allow this to happen. So, we need to look beyond leaders to make the world a greater place for every living soul. We need to take a long, hard look at ourselves and think beyond the usual question: what can I do? That question typically leads to few changes, like giving to charity or maybe voting differently (or even vote at all!). Although these are good on a superficial level, it's not the answer. It goes much deeper than that. We have to query how society functions, how we function within society, and what our role is on a grander scale.

I have lived in a part of the world where we are brought up with manners and respect, told to get a good education, land a good job, get married and have kids. There's nothing wrong with the above but often we become consumed by our lives and forget the bigger issues beyond our tunnel vision. With a good job, we make good money and start to enjoy the more materialistic side of life. Why? Simply because we can and it gives us instant satisfaction. We get promoted, receive a higher salary, and buy even more stuff we probably don't need. We purchase a house with a mortgage and work harder to pay it off. We get into an automatic frame of mind, satisfying ourselves with what we do and what we have gained. We constantly compare ourselves to others to satisfy our ego, and at the same time realize we just don't have enough. 'Trump can be President if it means lower taxes and I can keep more of my money'. Our conversations flit around our job, money, and what we spend it on. We stop reflecting and questioning. We fit perfectly into a self-involved society and climb the ladder laid out for us. We live what my artist friend, Tilo Kaiser, calls the catalogue life. We buy what is expected, that which gives us status and which we misinterpret for self-worth, and what impresses our neighbors and friends. It's an easy life based on the belief that titles and things make us happy. It's a life where we do not have to look around, reflect, or question anything. It's a life where we are doing, rather than being –

chasing rather than enjoying. It's a life that places the world in trouble and ensures it underperforms, and it does not give us happiness. We believe it does which makes it easy. If a fancier car or handbag can give us happiness, there is always something we can do to earn more money to buy it and, voila, we are happy. But that's not how life works. Studies have proven the above, and my personal experience in getting to know many multi-millionaires and billionaires, who have more money than they can spend, illustrates over and over that they're not happier than people from different walks of life. I'm not happier today than I was when I was a poor student, and this is scary. If titles and money do not give us happiness, what does? What can I do differently to become happy and stop these unconscious desires for things and titles that will never fully satisfy me?

What about marriage, why do we still carry out this tradition? I married my wife as she was the most important person in my life. I loved her greatly and couldn't imagine a life without her. I was convinced I would never divorce. But today I am. The divorce rate is around 50%; but that doesn't mean the other 50% who stay married are happy. Some of them might be but many are not. Look around you and you see couples that are together, hardly talking nor looking at each other. I can bet you anything that they're a married couple – guaranteed! They might have married because of love but they aren't staying together because of love. They stay together because they're married. I'm not judging if that's good or bad but simply making the point that it might not be rational if they want to be happy. Society expects us to stay together, and I know from personal experience it can be uncomfortable to state one is divorced – many friends include or exclude you because of that fact. If we look at a woman in her 40s with no kids, we judge her as if she's failed because we have been programmed to believe that women should follow the traditional path and have kids, so what's wrong with her that she decided to choose differently?

My point is not whether one should marry or not, have kids or not, but simply to point out that many things we do are based on how society has programmed us. We are greatly influenced in how we actually live out our lives, what opinions we have, and how these opinions were formed, and what impresses our friends and strangers alike. All to satisfy our ego. Our ego strives for superiority over others, it strives for instant gratification, for acceptance, and we spend our lives trying to satisfy our ego rather than living *our* life as we see fit. Earlier, I explained the ego is a major detriment in business, but it's also hazardous in our private lives. Your ego can control your thoughts, your fears, your needs, your desires; and worst of all, you simply follow it.

Today, you can't look around without seeing books about mindfulness and conscious living. There are new books coming out every day and it's a huge trend but what does it mean and what is it? The basic idea is that you try to be conscious of how your ego plays you, be mindful about which thought you allow your brain to entertain, and which ones you should avoid. I read a scientific study stating that consciousness can significantly reduce fears, among other things. What does that mean? Well, we all have fears and they occupy our mind. Some of you might be fearful of getting sick, some of you might worry you're never getting married. Some obsess about losing their job or perhaps you are dreading your next flight. These fears occupy your mind and might even give you sleepless nights where you toss in bed, obsessing about your fear. I've had moments in my life where I experienced this myself. You recall my setting up my bank earlier. It almost ruined me initially, made me physically ill and placed me in a terrible mood (according to my wife). I worried day and night for six months until it finally succeeded. But remember, such fears are simply thoughts. It's nothing more than thoughts, just like any other you might be having right now (perhaps your next dream vacation). Do we have a choice in choosing our thoughts, or somehow being able to focus less on those which can effectively ruin our quality of life? This is where consciousness and mindfulness enter the discussion. We don't have to entertain any thought that enters our brain; we actually have a choice! You cannot, unless highly trained, stop thoughts from entering your mind, but you can be conscious about the thoughts that enter and decide if you would like to entertain them. You have the power to ensure your thoughts are not controlling you. Imagine if your thoughts were a friend: if you lose your job you cannot pay your bills, and you would lose your home and end up on the street; or the plane you're travelling on might crash and you die. Would you keep such a pessimistic, depressing friend around? A friend that constantly fuels negative thoughts and your worst fears. Of course not! You would tell them to shut up or get lost but you don't chastise your own mind. Why? You believe you are your thoughts and fears. The great news? You are not your thoughts, and it's up to you to decide if you want to entertain them or not. It's not as easy as it sounds but it's quite amazing when you start practicing this.

When you were a little child, you were at your most authentic. You did whatever you wanted without worrying what others thought of it. You spoke honestly and truly without fear of social norms. You would fart, scream, cry, and do silly things simply because you felt like it. You didn't know then that society had decided what is right and wrong, acceptable and unacceptable. However, you were soon set on the 'acceptable' path. What you could do, when, what not, how to 'behave' etc. Of course, not all of these norms are a bad thing – there are certain standards to make a society work but it goes much further. We live our lives according to scripts and clear rules which have killed our natural instincts, honesty, and authenticity. If we see someone speaking freely or going against the normal rules of behavior, we label them crazy. These individuals are few and far between because most of us have adapted to the standards and live the life expected of us – steered by the ego because we want acceptance. Our ego craves acceptance so we try belonging to organizations, parties, religions, the cool crowd, or whatever. Look at the roots of nationalism. Borders are somewhat random and have been changing over time, but we cling to them. If our local football team plays against the neighboring team, we rally for our local team. If our country plays against another country, we rally for our country. If our region plays against another region, we rally for our region. All this despite the fact that we probably don't know any of the players. It's an emotional longing to satisfy our need to belong and, because it's emotional, it's easy to exploit by politicians or anybody else. Look at what Hitler achieved and you will understand what I mean. Hitler pronounced the German race as superior, in need of protection and expansion, and it needed to rule the world. It's amazing that a great number of the population jumped on that bandwagon, certainly not a sign of consciousness. Psychologists have demonstrated that most human decisions are based on emotions rather than rational analysis. Although that might have been good 1,000 years ago, today it is troubling. It often makes us 'follow the crowd' rather than deciding individually. Add to that the fact that humans prefer power over truth, and we have a very worrisome picture, explaining how Hitler could do it.

We are born as totally individual, naturally authentic human beings but are soon molded into 'good' citizens that are less reflective of our personalities and how we would like to live our lives (assuming you're not a psychopath). This suits our ego because the ego can play the 'good' citizen game very well. We strive to make ourselves feel important, smarter, better, richer, and more successful than others, and it gives us huge satisfaction when we have small victories: a bigger car than the neighbor, a better education, a finer house, a better job. If we fail to get ahead of someone, we put them down instead, 'Yes, he has that car but he inherited his money' or 'he only got into that school because of his dad'. We might not even realize we're doing this at all but our ego knows it. Measuring us against another undermines who we really are. Trying to catch up with your ego (and the Joneses) is a big problem – your greed will never be satisfied as there is always something bigger or better that 'they' have over you. McKinsey concluded in a study that basically reported what we already know:

whatever you have is (perceived) not enough. They asked people who had $100,000 and they stated if they had $500,000, it would be enough. They asked people who had $500,000 and they stated if they had $1 million, it would be enough. They asked people who had $1 million and they stated if they had $5 million, it would be enough. It carried on like that and was even true for billionaires who also wanted 'just one level higher'. That really says it all in a nutshell: no matter how much you have, you will want more, meaning we are not conscious of how our thoughts and ego drive our lives. That means we end up wanting a lot and spend our life trying to get it, until we die and look back and ask ourselves: was that really my life?

Most readers will argue 'but I am conscience and living my life in a conscientious way'. Well, I would argue most of you are wrong, which is why we have inequality, among other issues. Let's try to make the link.

If we live unconsciously (caught up in our own world), there are many things we won't reflect on, or even worse, reflect wrongly on or completely bypass. Look at our reactions to seeing poverty on TV. It's easy right? As we watch, we say or think 'oh, those poor people, how sad' and that's the extent of our thought process. We don't reflect on why they are poor. Instead we switch to a website to buy some more stuff. We don't even question if we feel entitled, but we do feel entitled otherwise we *could not* accept things as they are. The Western world feels entitled to a better life than those in the developing or third world nations. We feel it's absolutely OK to have several cars, nice houses, and more. We don't reflect on how amazingly wrong this narrow and selfish viewpoint is. The biggest factor in how well you can live in this world is determined by one single factor: where you are born. If you are born into a good, middle class family in Norway, you have a safe and rich life. If you are born in Somalia, you are 99% likely to struggle for basic things all your life. Birth can be likened to a lottery: you win or lose by birth. There is no equal opportunity on a global basis, none at all and we shouldn't feel entitled. Feeling entitled means we believe our life is more worthy than another soul and that doesn't sound right, does it? You see the news where 233 people have been killed by a bomb in Afghanistan and you barely shrug your shoulders. But if you hear three people got shot in your country, it literally hits you – because it could have been you. It was someone entitled and you are entitled, so what's going on? Perhaps a big discussion will break out about how this could happen, what's to be done, and it will go on for a long time. This is in sharp contrast to the three seconds of sorrow you felt when 233 people died in a bomb blast in Afghanistan. For many, fear now takes over and when a populist politician starts to label the Afghan people as dangerous and say that they shouldn't be allowed to enter the country, you are likely to agree. Why? Because you're not consciously reflecting but reacting and allowing that fear to guide your mind and opinions. This *is* the problem and this must change. Our lack of consciousness is being exploited by politicians and our fears emerge as racism in all forms and colors. Trump is a perfect example of this, stoking up fears and telling Americans they are above and beyond other world citizens, whom he is happy to call names and judge based on his personal prejudices. Those people who do not have a great (or any) capacity for reflection of truth and life, blindly and happily jump on it. Their egos enjoy seeing a guy like Trump 'fight' for 'their rights' even if it means destroying policies and institutions that have kept the world safe and made it richer over the last few decades. Trump himself is not the problem, rather the people who elected him and do not live conscious and reflective lives are a threat to world peace.

The discussions around climate change and Brexit are clear signs there is something fundamentally wrong with our society and with us. If we lived our lives more conscious of others, and understood how our ego plays us, we would be much more reflective and receptive to what really matters. We could consciously pursue a happiness independent of external influences. We would see that what really makes us happy is to be at peace with ourselves, accept ourselves as we are, and create meaningful relationships with others. This would help us to become more empathetic and to enjoy helping others; it would give us less time and need to hate or be mad at others, to want revenge, or try to pursue other negative forces. We would simply focus on what makes us happy. We have a right to pursue our own happiness and conscious living is the easiest way. Greed, racism, manipulation, and other negative traits would not consume us, instead we would fully enjoy other positive-conscious people and build a better world where war and the similar would have no place. I know this might sound a tad naive or spiritual but try thinking about it for a second. Look at yourself and your life, and reflect on how you live. What makes you really happy? What gives you stress? What drives you down the path to bad thoughts? Being human means, we will always struggle between giving in to our ego and doing the right thing, but the more we reflect, the less we manipulate ourselves and others, the better off we and the world will be. It's tragic that the greatest part of human suffering is not due to natural disasters, but is inflicted by humans on one another.

The people I grouped as 'spiritual' earlier are simply mindful people living consciously. They're conscious of the role their ego plays, conscious of the thoughts they (choose) to have, and mindful in general of how they interact with others. By doing so, they have no need to prove themselves to others but can simply focus on being at peace and happy with themselves. They are awake, reflective, and open to everything. They don't judge others and thereby put others down, nor do they feel entitled. These are not the kinds of people who typically start wars, are racists, or accept inequality. They don't waste their precious time '*Keeping Up with the Kardashians*' or paying heed to any kind of gossip, but if you engage them in a discussion about humanity, you will have their full attention.

Now imagine if the world were populated with these types of people. Trump would not be in office, Brexit would likely have never happened (and perhaps the EU would be a well-functioning institution), handling climate change would be steered by scientists and experts instead of wealthy individuals and companies, and inequality, I would argue, would never have reached the level it has. As stated earlier, the world has enough for everybody's needs, but there is not nearly enough for everybody's greed.

As humans, we will always innovate, create, develop, and build and that's a good thing. If we do it consciously rather than subconsciously and egocentrically, it will benefit a much larger group rather than just the wealthy elite. Eckhart Tolle mentions a human evolution where an awakening process takes place in which we all become more conscious. He argues that diminishment of the ego will give rise to empathy and compassion beyond tribal, racial, national, or religious affiliation, and if that happened, the world would be a significantly better place for all.

So as to the YOU in this book, this is what you could consider. Are you ready to break your subconscious pattern and start living consciously? You might or might not but, either way, to solve the world's problems, we need to embrace different discussions and view things differently if we hope to progress. I have been inspired by many great people and I hope you will have the same luck. Maybe what we actually need the most is strong leaders that inspire this conscious change in all of us. If great leaders lead us to become more conscious, it could have a profound ripple effect for all things discussed in this book. In an ever-increasingly conscious world, there would be fewer self-serving assholes and corrupt politicians. And politicians might not be able to cater to populistic ideas but actually focus on real solutions to real problems, such as income inequality. And the great business leaders will better cater to the need for businesses to not just serve their owners but the broader society.

So, with that thought, I would hope that great leaders of the world will step up and start that 'conscious' evolution, which in essence would mean WE ALL eventually step up. As John Lennon once sang:

*Imagine there's no countries*

*It isn't hard to do*

*Nothing to kill or die for*

*And no religion, too*

*Imagine all the people*

*Living life in peace*

*You may say I'm a dreamer*

*But I'm not the only one*

*I hope someday you will join us*

*And the world will be as one*

*Imagine no possessions*

*I wonder if you can*

*No need for greed and hunger*

*A brotherhood of man*

It's time…

# ABOUT THE AUTHOR

Mr. Nyholm is a seasoned senior executive turned entrepreneur. He grew up in Denmark but left for New York after his studies. Through his corporate career he's moved across borders 10 times and today lives in Switzerland. He has held senior positions in the financial services industry, most recently serving on the Executive Board of Credit Suisse through its three-year turn-around, before turning entrepreneur in 2004. As an entrepreneur, he set out to make banking an honorable business again, firstly by founding a consulting firm through which he advised the senior executives of some of Europe's largest banks and firms. With the 2008 financial crisis, where the classical banking model failed, he decided to set up his own bank. As a banker, he helped entrepreneurs and developed an interest in technology and digital businesses. With this passion, he joined one of his clients to help build a global Venture Capital firm, bringing technologies and entrepreneurship to multiple emerging markets, and he has been instrumental in developing a leading Blockchain firm that has set out to enable world-changing applications. With his wife he set up the Future4Children charity organization and he is supporting a middle American country through an Honorary Consul role. He holds an MBA from Columbia University, New York and a Bachelor degree in Economics from the Copenhagen Business School.

# NOTES AND REFERENCES

# PART II

## Notes

### CHAPTER 13:

[1] www.fastcompany.com/3004914/5-characteristics-great-leaders

[2] www.inc.com/peter-economy/the-9-traits-that-define-great-leadership.html

[3] www.fastcompany.com/1841916/how-properly-define-great-leader-and-act-one

[4] www.thebalancesmb.com/leadership-definition

### CHAPTER 16:

[1] www.theguardian.com/politics/2013/dec/06/conservative-party-uncomfortable-nelson-mandela

[2] www.brandsouthafrica.com/play-your-part-category/mandela-day-month/67minutes

[3] twitter.com/realDonaldTrump/status/1181232249821388801?s=20

## CHAPTER 17:

[1] Gilbert, Martin (1991). Churchill: A Life. London: Heinemann.

[2] Churchill, Winston (1989). *The Second World War*. London: Penguin.

# References

www.ranker.com/crowddranked-list/the-most-important-leaders-in-the-world

www.forbes.com/2012/11/21/are-leaders-born-or-made

www.thefamouspeople.com/profiles/william-henry-gates

www.biographyonline.net/business/bill-gates

www.biography.com/people/bill-gates

www.hubpages.com/business/Ingvar-Kamprads-leadership-style

www.theguardian.com/business/2018/jan28/ingvar-kamprad-obituary

www.astrumpeople.com/ingvar-kamprad-biography

www.thefamouspeople.com/profiles/ingvar-kamprad

www.wikipedia.org/wiki/ingvar_kamprad

www.forbes.com/sites/walterloeb/2012/12/05/ikea-is-a-world-wide-wonder

www.wikipedia.org/wiki/nelson_mandela

www.biography.com/people/nelson-mandela

www.wikipedia.org/wiki/winston_churchill

www.givingpledge.org

# PART III

## Notes

### CHAPTER 19:

[1] www.cdc.gov/mmwr/preview/mmwrhtml/mm4838a2.htm

[2] www.oxfam.org/en/press-releases/billionaire-fortunes-grew-25-billion-day-last-year-poorest-saw-their-wealth-fall

[3] www.cnbc.com/2018/01/22/oxfam-report-in-2017-there-was-a-new-billionaire-every-2-days.html

[4] www.worldbank.org/en/news

### CHAPTER 21:

[5] www.mckinsey.com/featured-insights/future-of-work/

[6] www.brookings.edu/blog/techtank/2018/04/18/will-robots-and-ai-take-your-job

### CHAPTER 22:

[7] www.pewresearch.org/Internet/2017/05/03/the-future-of-jobs-and-jobs-training/

[8] www.weforum.org/docs/WEF_Future_of_Jobs_2018.pdf

[9] www.mckinsey.com/featured-insights/future-of-work

http://www.mckinsey.com/featured-insights/future-of-work

## Chapter 24:

10 www.occrp.org

# References

Don Tapscott, Alex Tapscott, Blockchain Revolution

www.hackernoon.com

www.forbes.com/sites/bernardmarr/the-complete-beginners-guide-to-artificial-intelligence

www.forbes.com/sites/joemekendrick/2018/08/14

www.stopad.io/blog/artificial-intelligence-facts

www.singularityhub.com/2019/01/01/ai-will-create-millions-more-job

Thomas Piketty, Capital in the Twenty-First Century

Yuval Noah Harari, 21 Lessons for the 21st Century

www.forbes.com/2019/05/06/how-to-solve-americas-100-trillion-problem-of-wealth-inequality

www.artificialintelligence-news.com/2018/01/11/ai-wealth-inequality/

The Economist, 8.22.2019

The Economist, 17.8.2019

www.oxfam.org/en/even-it/paradise-papers-hidden-costs-tax-dodging

www.financialsecrecyindex.com

www.highcloud.io/how-ai-can-help-alleviate-poverty

www.iotforall.com/impact-of-artificial-intelligence-job-losses

www.sciencemag.org

www.edition.cnn.com/2019/07/30/business/future-education-technology

# PART III

## References

Eckhart Tolle, A new earth

Michael A. Singer, The untethered soul